T0328592

Cambridge Elements ≡

Elements in Environmental Humanities
edited by
Louise Westling
University of Oregon
Serenella Iovino
University of North Carolina at Chapel Hill
Timo Maran
University of Tartu

AGING EARTH

Senescent Environmentalism for Dystopian Futures

Jacob Jewusiak
Newcastle University

Shaftesbury Road, Cambridge CB2 8EA, United Kingdom

One Liberty Plaza, 20th Floor, New York, NY 10006, USA

477 Williamstown Road, Port Melbourne, VIC 3207, Australia

314–321, 3rd Floor, Plot 3, Splendor Forum, Jasola District Centre,
New Delhi – 110025, India

103 Penang Road, #05–06/07, Visioncrest Commercial, Singapore 238467

Cambridge University Press is part of Cambridge University Press & Assessment,
a department of the University of Cambridge.

We share the University's mission to contribute to society through the pursuit of
education, learning and research at the highest international levels of excellence.

www.cambridge.org
Information on this title: www.cambridge.org/9781009318365

DOI: 10.1017/9781009318372

First published 2023

A catalogue record for this publication is available from the British Library.

ISBN 978-1-009-31836-5 Paperback
ISSN 2632-3125 (online)
ISSN 2632-3117 (print)

Aging Earth

Senescent Environmentalism for Dystopian Futures

Elements in Environmental Humanities

DOI: 10.1017/9781009318372
First published online: July 2023

Jacob Jewusiak
Newcastle University
Author for correspondence: Jacob Jewusiak, jacob.jewusiak@newcastle.ac.uk

Abstract: Alarmist demography often situates older people as natural disasters: images of the "gray flood" and "silver tsunami" imbue senescence with the destructive force of climatic proportions. This Element focuses on the demographic dread arising from the relative shift in younger and older populations: not of a world lacking children, but of one catastrophized by the overabundance of the old and aging. Drawing on examples of science fictional sterility dystopias, *Aging Earth* challenges the privilege of youth in ecocritical thought and practice, especially the heteronormative urgency to address climate change for the sake of children and future generations. By decoupling the figurative connection between futurity and children, senescent environmentalism attunes itself to the contingency of non-linear and non-teleological futures: drawing together the delicacy of ecosystems on the brink with the structural precarity of older people, queers, and people of color.

Keywords: age, Anthropocene, dystopia, sexuality, race

ISBNs: 9781009318365 (PB), 9781009318372 (OC)
ISSNs: 2632-3125 (online), 2632-3117 (print)

Contents

Introduction

In September 2019, police arrested a 91-year-old man for blocking traffic on the A20 near Dover as part of an Extinction Rebellion protest against rising global temperatures and food insecurity. He told the reporter Emma Birchley that "the reason he was in Dover was because it was his generation that had caused the damage that led to climate change." His internalized guilt reflects a popular strand of environmentalist rhetoric that exploits generational tensions.[1] These tensions resonate in António Guterres's (2019) speech (in his capacity as United Nations Secretary-General) at the Youth Climate Summit: "My generation has largely failed until now to preserve both justice in the world and to preserve the planet." Yet this narrative of a "guilty" generation relies upon stereotypes that situate older people as a homogenous group, careless of how their consumption habits impact the planet. In contrast, media coverage on climate change centers younger people as both activists and victims: Guterres continues by addressing youth, "It is your generation that must make us [older people] be accountable to make sure that we don't betray the future of humankind." For many, the urgency of climate change arises from the way it renders the future precarious for children alive and yet unborn;[2] in this narrative, older people tend to occupy the position of either the unscrupulous villain or the guilty ally. Where the unspent years of youth take the symbolic form of futurity, the accumulated years of the older person stand in for a past that continues to exert toxic agency over the present and future. Bill McKibben, the founder of the activist group for individuals over sixty called Third Age, rationalizes his demonstrations against bank investment in fossil fuels as a form of generational reparation: "If you're 65 now, you've been on this planet for something like 80 percent of the carbon dioxide that's ever been emitted.... There's a debt to be paid, and there are ways to pay it" (Joselow). Suffused with the negative connotations of decline, older people take the fearsome shape of our extractive modernity, forming the planetary commons into the image of their own senescence. Now, both the planet and the older agents of environmental ruin share a dystopian fate, poised before the imminence of extinction.

Situating older people as the cause of the climate crisis draws on a long history of alarmist demography that represents older people as natural disasters.

---

[1] If an older person receives media attention for activism, age often overwhelms the message. The headline from the Sky News account of the Dover arrest – "Extinction Rebellion: 91-year-old climate protester arrested near port of Dover" – arises from the sensationalized incongruity of a 91-year-old in custody rather than the content of the protest or controversy about method.

[2] On the United Nations website, they observe that "Climate change has increased levels of uncertainty about our future. As its impacts intensify over time, one thing has become certain: We will leave the Earth to today's children and young people, and to future generations."

Age studies scholars such as Margaret Cruikshank (2009: 26–7) note the use of "disaster metaphors" such as the "flood," "avalanche," "tsunamis," and "icebergs" to stoke fear of an aging "society that lies just ahead." Drawing on the figure of the "grey tsunami" of older people in recent journalism, Andrea Charise (2012: 3) writes,

> This ominous rhetoric of rising, swamping, tides, and disease – amplified by the authoritative tones of medical and health policy expertise – conceives of population aging as an imminent catastrophe. Conceived en masse, the elderly are naturalized as a liquid cataclysm whose volume exceeds the nation's ability to contain, or even guard against, an abstracted human burden.

Older people have come to take on the destructive force of geologic and climatic proportions. Proscribed from the narrative of modern development as a burden, older people are, nevertheless, represented as a return of the repressed: the rising sea level made flesh. As a demographic group, older people absorb our collective ecological guilt: the threat of older age to progress, modernity, and capital paradoxically takes on the symbolic form of the environmental impacts of the processes they are imagined forestalling.

This figuration of older people as natural disasters gains force, in part, by the pervasive belief that our current climate crisis is a result of the depredations of previous generations. The imagery of tsunamis and floods registers the belief that older people are the greedy architects of the coming apocalypse, careless of a future planet that they will not experience. Research on the relations between older age and climate change sometimes reproduces this bias. A report from the Stockholm Environmental Institute (Haq, Brown, and Hards 2010: v) reports that "While older people are concerned about climate change, they do not feel they will be directly affected. Nor do they feel they can personally take action to stop it." Baby boomers, they note, "have the highest carbon footprint of any other age group" at 13.5 CO_2 tons/per capita while seniors (between the ages of sixty-five and seventy-four) have the second highest at 12.9 CO_2 tons/per capita (3). The discourse of climate change contributes to an idiomatic form of alarmist demography regarding older people: the size of their carbon footprint translates the demographic block into the disasters they are imagined causing.

Yet even as older people are posited as the cause and imaginatively take the shape of the disaster, they are also registered as vulnerable. In the same report from the Stockholm Environmental Institute, the authors note, "Older people may be physically, financially and emotionally less resilient to the effects of climate change" (v). Another report, "Climate Change in an Ageing World" (Byrne et al. 2015: 4), suggests that older people are often the first victims of environmental disasters:

Older people tend to experience greater impacts from flood events and a greater incidence of flood-related disease and higher rates of mortality. Floods often result in higher mortality rates among older people than other age groups due to direct causes such as drowning, in addition to secondary health impacts, such as hypothermia and heart problems.... There is growing evidence from national disaster loss data that older people are disproportionately more likely to die as a result of typhoons due to mobility difficulties, lack of evacuation assistance and inappropriate evacuation facilities, and disrupted access to essential health and medical support.

The representation of older people as cause and embodiment of climate catastrophe overlaps with their vulnerability to the environmental conditions they are accused of creating. While the tendency toward blame and vulnerability are not logically incompatible, this dynamic has given rise to a cultural narrative that frames older people as the instigator of intractable social and economic problems. The recriminatory structure of feeling that arises from this cultural framing – a deep sense of unfairness across generations, grudging allocation of welfare for "guilty" seniors, and a bitter sense of having to clean up someone else's mess – positions older people as a destructive force that threatens the integrity of the planet as a whole.[3]

To some, the potential future that younger people ·stand to lose with a changing climate justifies the stigmatization of older people: if it takes the creation of a scapegoat to energize public opinion and policy, so be it. Others might not go so far but remain suspicious of a demographic group with less "skin in the game" than the younger generation. Martha Nussbaum and Saul Levmore (2017: 190) remain tethered to a problematic model of generational warfare that stereotypes older people as incapable of sympathizing with the future: "Climate change policy is about aging in the sense that questions of intergenerational equity can pit aging citizens against younger ones. The disasters that are projected by climate change modes are by and large things that someone now in his or her sixties will not experience. It is no wonder that schoolchildren care much more about the topic than do members of their grandparent's generation." While acknowledging the importance of experience-based commitments, I cannot agree with what, in my view, devalues the lives of older people by linking their imaginative and sympathetic potential to the time they are expected to live. As I note above, older people receive blame for rising temperatures while they are also vulnerable to the global effects of a changing

---

[3] The ageism that pervades contemporary culture evolved from a nineteenth-century idiom of Malthusian scarcity where older people were imagined to parasitically sap the vitality of the social body. In *The Aesthetics of Senescence*, Andrea Charise (2020: xxv) suggests that "After Malthus, aging began to acquire an unfamiliar biopolitical overlay" that "recast aging as a *state* of life, fluid and unstable, and inseparable from the broader health and future of society."

climate. If we do not accept these as sufficient reasons for informing one's politics at an experiential level, then we unfairly stigmatize or infantilize older people based on our own unacknowledged ageist prejudices. By failing to take seriously the relation between older age and the environment, scholars participate in the denialism of a Western cult of youth that privileges strength, virility, fertility, family values, individualism, and ableism.[4] Thus, when the figure of youth occupies the cynosure of environmental reform, it tends to draw the cultural values of youth into a sphere of protection when these values are, in fact, the ones most in need of critique. Thus, I propose a senescent environmentalism to critique the manifold ways that youth shapes the teleology of environmental reparation and recuperate older age as a life stage that inspires alternative models of futurity.

In her work situating old age as a cultural construct, the age studies scholar Margaret Gullette (2004: 13) argues that decline ideology has shaped the "authoritative narrative" about the process of growing old. The decline narrative emphasizes subtraction over time: strength is replaced by weakness and frailty, memory with forgetfulness and disorientation, youthful beauty with wrinkles and mottled skin. "[D]ecline's emphasis," she writes, "falls like a bludgeon on what excludes old people from the human majority: weakness, closeness to mortality" (2017: 13). Opposed to the hegemony of decline, Gullette (2004: 17) proposes associating older age with the "progress narrative," or "stories in which the implicit meanings of aging run from survival, resilience, recovery, and development, all the way up to collective resistance to decline forces." Gullette's arguments about age resonate with what Ursula Heise (2016: 8) has called "the environmentalist rhetoric of decline." By this she refers to "the idea that modern society has degraded a natural world that used to be beautiful, harmonious, and self-sustaining and that might disappear completely if modern humans do not change their way of life" (7). In contrast to Gullette, Heise resists turning to the rhetoric of "progress boosterism": "Is it possible to acknowledge the realities of large-scale species extinction and yet to move beyond mourning, melancholia, and nostalgia to a more affirmative vision of our biological future?" (12, 13). Both Gullette's work on older age and Heise's work on the extinction of non-human species attests to a shared investment in narrative and time: though they function at vastly different scales, the narrative we use to shape the arc of a human life draws upon the same structural and ideological conventions as the narrative we use to represent the planet.

---

[4] I appreciate the feedback from the anonymous reader of this manuscript, who encouraged me to engage more deeply with the status of youth in Western culture.

The concerns of age studies have remained largely distinct from the concerns of the environmental humanities.[5] The lack of intersection arises, in part, from a mismatch of scale and time. Where youth occupies a privileged place in the environmental imaginary, urging us to act quickly on climate change to ensure that all young people will have a place to dwell in the future, age studies urges our attention to the overlooked experience of older age and the life course as a whole. Where age studies scholars tend to focus on more immediate institutional and domestic contexts – the intersubjective space of the care home, the latent ageism of medical triage, the inaccessibility of our homes and social spaces – ecocritics often use the analysis of a specific instance as a means of addressing problems on a massive scale: the impact of human intervention on millions of years of geological development, the acceleration of mass extinctions, the effects of climate change on the livelihood of marginalized people across the globe. In bringing the two disciplines into dialogue around narrative, this Element grapples with the productive dissonance that arises when the timescales of human aging and the planet briefly overlap. How does the intimate experience of growing older inform the way we understand the macrocosmic timescale of the planet? How does environmentalist discourse conjure urgency by framing the warming planet as decrepit and frail, metaphorically near the end of life? Can a senescent environmentalism help us to articulate new solutions to the manifold problems afflicting our planet?

To answer these questions that arise at the intersection of age and the environment, I focus on the sterility dystopia: a subgenre of science fiction where a global inability to have children results in aging populations and societal collapse.[6] Though usually not specified intradiegetically, the cause of universal infertility is tacitly connected to human influence: industrial pollution, genetic manipulation, nuclear testing, and so on. Significant works in the genre include Cousin de Grainville's *The Last Man* ([1805] 2002), Brian Aldiss's *Greybeard* ([1964] 2011), Margaret Atwood's *The Handmaid's Tale* ([1985] 1996), Octavia Butler's trilogy *Lilith's Brood* ([1987–9] 2007), P. D. James's

---

[5] Some recent scholarship has emerged at the intersection of age studies and ecocriticism, led by Kathleen Woodward. I discuss her (2020) article "Ageing in the Anthropocene" in my section "Queer Genre/ations" below, but she has also published an essay in 2022 titled "Old Trees Are Our Parents." Kristi McKim's (2022) "'Always the Same and Ever New': Clouds, Aging, and Climatology in *Clouds of Sils Maria*" also attests to a burgeoning interest in the possibilities that arise at the intersection of the two fields.

[6] The sterility dystopia is an aspect of what Andreu Domingo (2008: 725) has called the "demo-dystopias," or dystopias that make "demographic change or that make population matters a salient concern." His work helps to historicize the rise of the sterility dystopia: the "social definition of youth and old age radically changed during the twentieth century. Youth lasts longer; old age sets in later. ... These changes are reflected in the shifting treatment of youth and old age in the dystopias written over the decades since the 1960s" (733).

The Children of Men ([1992] 2018), and Louise Erdrich's *Future Home of the Living God* (2017). Arising from declining fertility rates and the specter of depopulation in advanced industrial nations, the sterility dystopia expresses the demographic fear arising from the relative shift in younger and older populations – not of a world lacking children, as we might expect, but of one catastrophized by the overabundance of the old and aging. Through its exploration of this demographic transformation, the novels in this genre tend to address the following: how to manage existential dread when confronting the lack of an anthropocentric future; how the bonds of society and political ideologies warp when confronted with demographic changes that disrupt the economic status quo; how crisis inspires the swift reversion to tyranny and prejudice. In contrast to other forms of writing on the demographics of the Anthropocene – ranging from popular non-fiction to scholarly articles and monographs – the sterility dystopia brings the reader into a thrilling anticipation of the end of humanity, giving imaginative shape to fears that might otherwise remain an amorphous, dull dread of imminent calamity.

The first section of this Element, "Revelations for an Aging Planet," traces a historical narrative that links anthropogenic climate change to the development of "modern" attitudes toward aging. Beginning in the nineteenth century, anxieties about a surplus older population contributed to and amplified fears about the scarcity of planetary resources. I suggest that the last-man narratives of Jean-Baptiste Cousin de Grainville and Mary Shelley represent an epochal shift in the imagination of how older age impacted the environment and set the groundwork for the sterility dystopias I analyze in the sections that follow. The second section, "Queer Genre/ations," examines the role of generational futurity in constructing existential and social value. While the passage of generations is one way to imagine temporal scale beyond the limits of the individual human lifespan, it also relies upon problematic heteronormative assumptions. Through a reading of P. D. James's *The Children of Men*, I argue that the sterility dystopia problematizes the future orientation of the science fiction genre by redirecting our attention to intergenerational kinship. Privileging contingency, extended immediacy, and temporal neutrality, intergenerational kinship contests the hegemony of generational futurity and challenges the slow, nearly invisible transformations that funnel "progress" to the privileged elite at the expense of marginalized groups. The third section, "Senescent Futurity," focuses on the role of temporality and reproduction in regimes of racialized, gendered, and environmental violence. Taking Louise Erdrich's *Future Home of the Living God* as a case study, I theorize a relational, kinship model of temporality that I call "senescent futurity," a relation to the future that draws upon Indigenous aging to activate our sense of care and responsibility – not only to marginalized older people as a living symbol of that futurity, but to the older self we might one day become.

In its attenuation of youth and generational progress, the sterility dystopia entangles the end of the world with the end of life: the reader grapples with their own fears about the future alongside the distraught characters. Yet these novels do more than conjure dread. My close readings reveal the genre's investment in critiquing the way Western culture sutures the future to the reproduction of youthful, able bodies. In asking us to reckon with a senescent futurity, the sterility dystopia reveals that the "Future" in peril is only one possible future among many. The genre subtly displaces its horror, which does not arise from the lack of children, but from the tyrannical coupling of children with futurity. This coupling works against the very "Future" of the liberal society that holds it dear, as the figure of the child rationalizes the accumulative drive ("to create a more prosperous future") more often than it inspires a reparative one ("to create a more sustainable future"). More horrifyingly, however, the coupling of children with futurity nullifies all other possible futures: senescent futures, queer futures, Indigenous futures. This Element draws on literature as a form where these impossible futures effervesce into alternative social configurations that offer the possibility of dwelling and aging in more sustainable ways. The sterility dystopia makes a senescent future visible by suspending the ability to conceive children: older age serves as the limit case for imagining a future poised before the end, which makes the genre a timely way to reconceptualize our collective orientation toward impending environmental catastrophe.

Revelations for an Aging Planet

In a 2000 article in the *Global Change Newsletter*, Paul Crutzen and Eugene Stoermer proposed the term Anthropocene to define a new geologic epoch where environmental change was driven by anthropogenic causes. Through industrial agriculture, the burning of fossil fuels, the release of chlorofluorocarbons into the atmosphere, and the destruction of ecosystems and concomitant extinction of species, humans have come to rival "some of the great forces of Nature in [our] impact on the functioning of the Earth system" (Crutzen et al. 2011: 843). Through these actions, humans have accelerated the process of global warming and triggered increasingly devastating climatic events: melting ice caps and rising sea levels, soaring temperatures, volatile and extreme weather, droughts in South Africa, wildfires across the west coast of the United States. The late eighteenth and early nineteenth centuries play an important role in Crutzen's and Stoermer's account, as they posit the beginning of the Anthropocene with James Watt's development of the steam engine in

1784.[7] But some scholars have questioned the Anthropocene concept, troubling both its historical narrative and the centrality of *anthropos* to the term: Jason Moore's (2015: 176) Capitalocene replaces a Eurocentric focus on "well-worn notions of resource- and technological-determinism" with the history of "the endless accumulation of capital" that began in the long sixteenth century. Donna Harraway's (2016b: 557) Plantationocene, which "makes one pay attention to the historical relocations of the substances of living and dying around the Earth as a necessary prerequisite to their extraction," also expands the historical narrative to the global networks of the sixteenth century. The Anthropocene and the other epoch making -ocenes that followed in its wake serve as interfaces for revealing the profound effects of certain humans (primarily white, male, capitalists) on the planet.

This section suggests that, alongside the anthropogenic focus on the industrial modernity of the nineteenth century, older populations were imbued with a newly devastating capacity to affect the functioning of society and, eventually, the planet as a whole.[8] For scholars of age, the nineteenth century marked a turning point in the cultural significance and institutional place of older age. Stephen Katz (1996: 76) writes that "pensions and retirement, and the social survey, together with the modern discourses of reform, the life-course regime, and alarmist demography" made the "elderly" newly visible "as an unproductive, dependent, and incapacitated population" (66). Older people became "a social problem requiring governmental response" (26). For Karen Chase (2009: 102), the Victorian drive to classify and define "old age" resulted in the nineteenth-century "invention of the elderly subject" – making the later years of life newly available for medical and juridical scrutiny. The new visibility of older age occurred against the backdrop of unprecedented demographic change as populations exploded across Europe: R. I. Woods (1996: 298) observes that from 1801 to 1901 the population in Britain grew from 8.8 million to over 32 million (for comparison, there was an estimated 4.4 million in 1601).

---

[7] As Jeremy Davies writes in *The Birth of the Anthropocene* (2016: 16), "three-tenths of the current CO2 level is attributable to the development of industrial society since the late eighteenth century." Timothy Morton (2013: 7) similarly attributes the beginning of the Anthropocene to 1784: "It was April 1784, when James Watt patented the steam engine, an act that commence the depositing of carbon in Earth's crust – namely, the inception of humanity as geophysical force on a planetary scale."

[8] It is essential to acknowledge the profound geographic unevenness of the Anthropocene. This social and economic organization of life toward ever-increasing productivity and consumption, which found an early, forceful expression in nineteenth-century Britain, found idiosyncratic forms across the globe and at different times. As the transition to an industrial economy radically reshaped attitudes toward human aging, resistance to this narrative was registered most strongly by non-Western and Indigenous people, who often retained stronger intergenerational links and societal roles for older people. I will go on to explore this in the section "Senescent Futurity" below.

Nicholas Daly (2015: 1, 4) writes that as "life for most people began to be longer and more predictable" "ageing and longevity become a recurring source of interest." The growth of older populations was also a source of irrational fear. While the population of older people increased over the course of the nineteenth century, the proportion of older people to young decreased.[9] Despite this demographic shift toward youth, older people – newly homogenized and subject to discourses of knowledge and power – became increasingly stigmatized as a non-productive burden on the economy.

A series of legislative and institutional changes in nineteenth-century British society both responded to and helped to shape the older population as a destructive demographic force. The most significant was the passage of the New Poor Law in 1834, which registered the fear that older people were burdens to society that stalled economic growth. In response to the problem of older age pauperism, the New Poor Law transitioned away from a system of outdoor relief (where funds were, sometimes, allocated to the "deserving" poor) to a centralized system where the older poor were deposited in workhouses. The workhouses, Pat Thane writes (2000: 166), were "embedded in the conscious-ness of poor people of all ages as pitiless 'bastilles'." As a deterrent against relying on state aid, the workhouses were a resounding success and after "1871 the percentage of people receiving poor relief (indoor and out, regular and irregular) fell" (171). Exiling the surplus older population to workhouses amplified the view of older people as a burden and drain to society, grafting the process of growing older onto a narrative of economic and environmental decline. Diana Coole (2012: 61) writes that

> Ideas about the nature of work, productivity and the life cycle that still structure definitions of the elderly were forged in an earlier era of industrial capitalism and are now arguably obsolete. It was in that context that new rituals, roles and identities associated with a specifically modern life cycle were constructed, alongside ... the distinction between productive and unproductive labour that has remained central to modern economics and to the problematization of aging ever since.

While the historical conditions that "modernized" aging have changed, the social institutions and cultural narratives that arose to account for growing older remain powerful realities, though they have evolved in relation to our present crises. Nineteenth-century discourse did not imbue older age with the sting of environmental blame and generational guilt that has characterized its

---

[9] Ina Ferris summarizes Malthus's anxieties about Ireland: "Quite literally, the margins of the nation begin to press on the centre, assuming a frightening gigantism, and the population-fact begins to exceed its strictly economic dimensions" (33).

representation in the twenty-first century. But the recriminatory structure of feeling has remained the same – translated from a nineteenth-century idiom of Malthusian scarcity where older people parasitically sapped the vitality of the social body to our current idiom of older people as a destructive force that threatens the integrity of the planet as a whole.

Thomas Malthus's *An Essay on the Principle of Population* (1798) plays an important role in this narrative of nineteenth-century demographics. In *The Aesthetics of Senescence*, Andrea Charise (2020: xxv) suggests that "After Malthus, aging began to acquire an unfamiliar biopolitical overlay" that "recast aging as a *state* of life, fluid and unstable, and inseparable from the broader health and future of society." Malthus's dire warnings of unchecked population growth – attributed, in part, to the moral failures of the working classes – also implied that youthful, reproductive bodies were to blame for demographic disaster: "Malthusian anxieties about population linked youth to an apocalyptic view of reproduction, viewing reproductive capacity less an antidote to national decline than its ominous, destructive wellspring" (34). Charise turns to Mary Shelley's *The Last Man* as a text that frames senescence as a "socially renovating" means of controlling youthful profligacy (53): "the recuperative potential of older age," Charise writes, "becomes the means by which community can be cultivated in the midst of the Malthusian crisis" (55–6). Contrasted against the youthful impulsivity and individualism that undergirds irrational population expansion, Shelley presents an image of older age that is "a viable, therapeutic, even consummate state of embodiment" that enables a sense of communal responsibility (35).

Building on Charise's work, this section takes a broader look at the proliferation of last-man narratives at the beginning of the nineteenth century, beginning with Cousin de Grainville's *The Last Man* and ending with Shelley's volume. These narratives set up the extinction of humanity against the backdrop of an environment that reflects (in the case of Grainville) or contrasts (in Shelley) the caducity of the species. In Grainville's depopulating world, universal infertility arises from the wrath of God and the depredations of human industry. The two remaining fertile people on earth are forced to make a choice – preserve the species or follow the will of God and trigger the apocalypse. While the latter choice results in the end of time and the extinction of all life, it allows the faithful dead to enjoy an eternal existence where temporal distinctions no longer signify. The planet – personified in the novel through the Spirit of the Earth – struggles for existence amid this battle between past and future generations. Though Shelley's *The Last Man* is not a sterility dystopia in the strict sense of the term, as human extinction arises from the plague rather than infertility, the novel deploys the themes of intergenerational dysfunction and premature senescence that inspire twentieth- and twenty-first century-dystopian writers. Where Grainville links the senescence of the planet with that of a species in decline, Shelley represents the flourishing of nature in spite of human extinction. As Shelley associates the dwindling population with the senescence of the human race, she contrasts this against a thriving and unsympathetic planet.

My readings of these last-man narratives challenge Charise's assertion of a salvific role of older age: though virile youth might be the villain in Malthus's narrative, it was senescence that, nevertheless, became increasingly stigmatized over the course of the nineteenth century. Non-reproductive older age does not serve as the means of overcoming the effects of overpopulation because both novels end with a depopulated planet: an absolute lack of humans is a poor solution to the problem of too many. Instead, these last-man narratives show how the irrational Othering of senescence acts as a self-destructive disavowal of the future. The novels scale this disavowal to the level of planetary apocalypse: rejecting the older self that one might become encodes, at the level of the individual, the larger anthropocentric assertion that humans are ontologically exceptional. Moreover, the state of exceptionality is inherently self-defeating: where the younger person represses care for her older self, the industrialist ignores the projected effects of his waste on the quality of the soil and air for future generations. Both older age and the environment are projected onto the temporal hinterlands of an Othered future, too distant in time and massive in scale to activate the sympathy and care that they require. While the last-man genre might be viewed as an affirmation of Greg Garrard's (2012: 59) claim that it is "the world with far fewer of us that we should seek to imagine, and to achieve," human depopulation is a side effect of a deeper interest in how shifts in demographic scale enable or disable sympathetic responses across time and space.[10] Written against the backdrop of an increasingly institutionalized marginalization of older age in the early nineteenth century, the last-man narratives map the demographic impacts of growing older onto an apocalyptic narrative of global scale and set the groundwork for the twentieth- and twenty-first-century sterility dystopias that I analyze in later sections.

---

[10] Scholars have pointed out that discourse about population size often entails dangers to marginalized groups. See, for example, Neel Ahuja's "Intimate Atmospheres" (2015), Catriona Sandiland's "Eco Homo" (2004), and Andil Gosine's "Non-White Reproduction and Same-Sex Eroticism" (2010). I will go on to discuss this issue at more length below, in the section "Senescent Futurity," in the context of Indigeneity, relationality, and aging. In Erdrich's bleak vision of future precarity, marginalized ethnic groups are among the first to suffer at the hands of a new repressive regime.

Lastness, Longevity, and Eternal Life

Published in France in 1805, Jean-Baptiste Cousin de Granville's *Le Dernier Homme* (*The Last Man*) inspired a transnational trend of dystopian last-man literature. The novel presents two competing narratives for the end of the world and humanity. The first relates to the liberal drive toward progress and improvement. Set in a future world of technological advancement, the very means that have enriched the human species have exhausted the planet's resources: "the earth had fallen victim to the common destiny: after struggling for centuries against the onslaught of time, and of men, she was exhausted and bore the sad features of decay" (9–10). The novel aligns the depredations of human industry with the aging of the human body as similarly enervating processes of decline. The other explanation for the end of the world is religious. According to God's plan, Earth has simply run out of time, like a watch that has been allowed to run down. Much of the narrative pivots on whether Omegarus, the last remaining fertile man on earth, will accept this divinely ordained ending or sire "the most accursed of all races" (93). As Omegarus chooses to abandon and thus destroy his wife and unborn child, God's plan for the end of the world comes to fruition: Earth and time are abolished in favor of an encompassing eternity. Though Grainville accords God apocalyptic agency, the scientific rationale about the exhaustion of planetary resources and demographic pressures of overpopulation remains a convincing counternarrative.

The primary symptom of impending apocalypse takes the form of declining birthrates and, eventually, near universal sterility. With the exception of Omegarus, no child had been born in Europe in the last twenty years: "France, like the rest of Europe, was a vast and empty realm. For twenty years before I was born, marriages had proved sterile. Men, as they grew old, with no children to the replace them, thought that the earth was seeing its last inhabitants" (14). The fecundity of both the earth and the human body are linked: as the dying sun slowly cools the earth, as the barren soil no longer draws forth the seed, the human body is likewise unable to produce offspring. The narrator connects this pervasive sterility to the inevitable degeneration that occurs once the pinnacle of perfection has been reached: "When earth had attained so high a degree of glory and of happiness, it began to experience the fate of humankind. Once they had arrived at the perfection of body and soul, the flame began to die within them. Chill old age and death followed. Earth, home to the happiest of mortals – a second Eden – began to lose its fertility" (34). Critics such as Henry Majewski (1963: 114) frame the novel's apocalypticism as a cynical "reaction to the contemporary philosophical doctrines of progress and the inevitable perfectibility of mankind." Writing in the aftermath of a bloody revolution and amid the proliferation of industry,

Grainville's disintegrating planet reflected his disillusionment with the ameliorative effects of rational modernity.[11]

Grainville embeds Malthus's narrative of scarcity into his dystopian tale to counteract the celebratory belief in perfectibility and progress. Before sterility afflicts both the planet and humankind, the world enters a golden age of peace and invention. The foremost of the great philosophers, Philantor, discovers "the secret of prolonging human life and of retarding the onset of old age" (30). However, before offering his cure to the general population, Philantor has Malthusian misgivings: "His fear was that, if he were to give mankind the means of prolonging life, the earth would not be capable of sustaining the huge numbers that would fill the globe . . . their too numerous descendants who would fight to the death for living space" (31). Instead, Philantor concocts enough serum to anoint only the most deserving benefactors of humankind, who receive their youth after winning a highly competitive global election. Where Philantor takes a passive approach to population control, prolonging life for only a select few, the personification of Death takes pride in the ecological benefits of its more active approach. In a conversation with the Spirit of Earth late in the novel, Death rejects the Earth's instincts of preservation:

> by shedding torrents of blood I have proved the greater benefactor of the human race. Had I not saved earth from an overabundance of children, they would have exhausted all her resources. I could have acted against you only by leaving them in the narrow space of this world where, crowded into every corner, they would have produced nothing, not even the barren weeds of the field. It was essential to slow down this growth of population, to destroy men in order to preserve the human race. (133)

While both Philantor and Death present their Malthusian arguments as the most rational means for human striving, their attempts at achieving a sustainable population in relation to the earth's resources ultimately fails. Fiona Stafford (1994: 205) writes that "Malthus' *Essay* might be undemocratic or indeed, positively inhumane, but it was at least directed toward the survival of the human race. Grainville's novel demonstrates that the best intentions of even the most noble human being serve only to destroy art, love, and the world itself." Exhaustion and decrepitude arrive for the human species and the planet regardless of the extreme measures to forestall it.

---

[11] Fiona Stafford writes: "When the French historian, Michelet, composed his *Histoire du XIX Siècle* in 1872–5, he isolated two books as representative of the despair of the first decade; one was Thomas Malthus' *Essay on the Principle of Population* and the other, *Le Dernier Homme*. Both were written in response to the 'grandes destruction d'hommes' which had begun under the combined influence of Napoleon and the Industrial Revolution, and both were preoccupied with starvation and sterility" (205).

In *The Last Man*, the inexorable march of the individual organism toward older age and death scales up to the level of the planet itself. This is more than a metaphor: Grainville asserts that the planet is old and on the verge of death. While God has the wisdom to perceive the effects of senescence and the necessity of death, the personified Spirit of the Earth rejects older age in a desperate quest to restore lost youthfulness and vitality. Like Death, Earth receives an avatar in *The Last Man* – in this form, the Spirit entreats Omegarus to travel from France to Brazil to discover the last remaining fertile woman, Syderia. The Earth's desperate attempt to preserve humans arises from God's promise to prolong the Earth's life as long as there are humans to sustain. As the human population dwindles, however, Earth ages: "'Earth!' [Adam] exclaimed, 'you whom I saw walking in beauty from the Creator's hands, where are your pleasant hills, your fields bright with flowers, your green bowers? You are a wasteland. Old age has dimmed the light of the sun itself whose brilliance we thought would never die'" (10).[12] Present at the first flush of creation and its end, Adam observes the wreckage of cosmic entropy, which he associates with the ravages of biological aging. Yet Adam's perspective offers an important distinction. Where the novel aligns the earth's aging with depopulation and the twilight of the species, Adam's presence draws attention to a corresponding human scarcity at the genesis of creation where, nevertheless, the fecund earth has resources to support a proliferating young species. While the novel connects depopulation with senescence, it also imaginatively links the states of older age and youth through a demographics of quantity. Both the beginning and the end of the human species are marked by the existence of very few humans on the earth.

While *The Last Man* asserts that the earth's longevity is predicated upon the reproduction of the human species, it also suggests that humans are the agents of planetary destruction: to cure the planet, there needs to be more of the very humans who caused the devastation in the first place.

> Like all created things the earth cannot last for ever. Nature has calculated the instant of its decline, and, like a good mother, she has prepared the means of regeneration. But earth has exceeded the time assigned by nature. Those she has nourished, on whom she has showered her gifts – her own children – will end by destroying her. From her generous hands, they received fruits in abundance, and yet their desires were never satisfied. From her womb, they have hastened to extract the very essence of her life. By taking too much from nature, they have been spendthrifts with their power and have squandered

---

[12] The narrator observes that the ambitious project to clear the ocean floor for human habitation is cut short by an abrupt transformation of the sun: "the sun began to show signs of old age: it grew pale, and its rays lost their heat" (40).

their inheritance. There remains but one remedy for such great evil – the union of Omegarus with the only woman who with him can ensure the continuance of the human race. (27)

Humans are simultaneously the disease and the remedy. Having exhausted the Earth's resources through reckless greed, the only solution, in the face of annihilation, is to reproduce the very anthropogenic blight that sterilized both the planet and human biology.[13] Though Grainville ultimately represents the triumph of God's alternative – total destruction as the means to salvation – the relation of humans to the Earth is deeply ambivalent throughout the text. In Jacques Derrida's (1981: 70) reading of Plato's *pharmakon*, he identifies how the two senses of the *pharmakon* – its signification as both poison and cure – presents a binary choice that obscures the indeterminacy and undecidability that inheres in the relation: "this 'medicine,' this philter, which acts as both remedy and poison, already introduces itself into the body of the discourse with all its ambivalence. This charm, this spellbinding virtue, this power of fascination, can be – alternately or simultaneously – beneficent or maleficent." Where Derrida analyzes writing as the *pharmakon*, for Grainville it is the human species which raises an undecidable ecological antimony: humans can be agents of either planetary destruction or reparation. Or both.

Grainville's novel frames humans as a *pharmakon* to the planet that they inhabit. "Apprehended as a blend and an impurity," Derrida writes,

> the *pharmakon* also acts like an aggressor or a housebreaker, threatening some internal purity and security.... The purity of the inside can then only be restored if the *charges are brought home* against exteriority as a supplement, inessential yet harmful to the essence, a surplus that *ought* never to have come to be added to the untouched plenitude of the inside. (128)

In the confusion between human-inflicted and divinely ordained extinction, Grainville unsettles one of the most fundamental and stubborn anthropocentric beliefs about human exceptionality.[14] Rather than center humans as an ontologically privileged species and the earth as its nourishing supplement, *The Last Man* inverts the narrative. Omegarus might be the titular last man, but the Spirit of Earth is the more sympathetic, Mephisthophelean protagonist; indeed, the

---

[13] This counterintuitive logic will be familiar to twenty-first-century reader, who has observed calls for economic and technological growth to augment our resources to combat the climate change caused from unrestricted growth.

[14] Derrida expands on the policing of inside and outside that occurs with supplementarity: "In order to cure the latter [*logos-zoon*] of the parasite, it is thus necessary to put the outside back in its place. To keep the outside out. This is the inaugural gesture of 'logic' itself, of good 'sense' insofar as it accords with the self-identity of *that which is*: being is what it is, the outside is outside and the inside inside. Writing must thus return to being what it *should never have ceased to be*: an accessory, an accident, an excess" (128).

novel ends with the epic battle between the Spirit of Earth and Death while the human apocalypse fades into the background. The resulting narrative is profoundly unsympathetic to human survival. Omegarus has, after all, abandoned his pregnant wife and consigned his fellow humans to destruction to fulfill God's wish, while the Spirit of the Earth struggles with Death itself to live: "The more centuries he lived, the less could the Spirit resign himself to death. Every second of his life increased his will to live" (130). While the narrative foregrounds the Earth's struggle for existence, humans – both necessary for the Earth's survival and yet the instrument of its destruction – are demoted into a supplementary role.

By inverting the reader's expectations about the ontological privilege of humanity over the earth, Grainville's *The Last Man* also disrupts other hierarchical categories. The most important in *The Last Man* is age, as older age symbolically registers the barrenness of the apocalyptic future. At times, the text's representation of senescence aligns with stereotypes of older age as a static, decrepit state. Yet the text also opens the possibility of interpreting this stage of life differently: as the philosopher Ormus reflects, "How many delightful hours have I passed here in pondering the wonders of Nature! I find her still beautiful even in her old age" (62). The novel gestures to the way the aesthetics of aging arise from deeply engrained fears about human biology. Decoupling human biology from the concept of aging, and thus displacing the harmful stigmas arising from mortality, gives rise to the counterintuitive beauty that Ormus perceives in the depopulating and sterile landscapes afflicted by the passage of time. The imminent apocalypse merely destroys the comforting anticipation that future generations will carry on the human legacy. Such is the affective force of generational futurity that Grainville cannot imagine the planet existing without its human *pharmakon*. While future sections will go on to develop this concept of generational futurity – attending to the way it intersects with issues relating to gender, sexuality, and race through contemporary science fiction – I turn now to Mary Shelley's *The Last Man*, which represents the thriving of the planet as a counterpoint to the excruciatingly slow death of the human species.

The Gray Plague

Set in the late twenty-first century, Shelley's *The Last Man* represents a familiar world to her early-nineteenth-century readership. While technological advancements have improved agriculture and modes of transport, the weapons of war and political crises (in particular, the conflict between Greece and Turkey) are all drawn from Shelley's contemporary milieu. The titular last man, Lionel

Verney, writes from the aftermath of the plague, wandering the earth in a lonely quest for human companionship. The effects of the plague, however, are only felt approximately midway through the novel: the charismatic and ambitious Raymond, married to Lionel's sister Perdita, abdicates his role as leader of England to command the Greek resistance against the Turks. Raymond's siege of Constantinople succeeds when the plague annihilates the population, allowing him to enter the city unmolested – though at the cost of his life. Plague eventually reaches England, resulting in mass death and terror. When the population reaches critically low levels, the new Protector of England – Lionel's friend Adrian – facilitates the emigration of the remaining thousands to the safer climates of France and Switzerland. Despite this last effort, their numbers continue to dwindle until only Lionel remains.

Written after the deaths of Shelley's friend Lord Byron, her husband Percy Bysshe Shelley, and her children Clara and William, *The Last Man* attests to the loneliness arising from her deep grief. In her journal from 1824, Shelley aligns her desolation with that of "The Last Man! Yes, I may well describe that solitary being's feelings: I feel myself as the last relic of a beloved race, my companions extinct before me": "All my old friends are gone," she writes, and a "new race is springing about me" (112–3, 114). Her feeling of belatedness takes the symbolic form of premature senescence: "At the age of twenty-six I am in the condition of an aged person" (114). For Shelley, older age registers the condition of living beyond the social connections that give one's life meaning. *The Last Man*'s relentlessly bleak vision of the future offers little hope for humanity. Even Shelley's *The Last Man* itself is a belated entry into the well-established last-man genre, which, as Morton Paley notes (1993: 107), "had come to seem not apocalyptic but ridiculous" by 1826.

Both Grainville's and Shelley's novels share a similar socio-historical narrative: the liberal drive toward progress and improvement has resulted in more peaceful and enlightened societies across the globe: in Shelley's words, "disease was to be banished; labour lightened of its heaviest burden" (106). Full of optimism, Adrian observes that "The energies of man were before directed to the destruction of his species: they now aim at its liberation and preservation . . . poverty will quit us, and with that, sickness" (219). Yet at the highest point of perfection the bottom falls out: once human society reaches this pinnacle, when the imagination is no longer capable of pushing on to better possibilities, collapse is swift and encompassing. The only inconceivable temporality is stasis: "'All things go on,' thought Perdita, 'all things proceed, decay, and perish! . . . All proceeds, changes and dies'" (135). While the last-man genre is dystopian in its representation of global human extinction and the breakdown of society, it is also anti-utopian in its anxiety about the stasis arising from societal perfection. For both Grainville and Shelley, such utopian hubris is met with a bloody reversal of fortunes.

Yet Shelley's narrative differs from Grainville's in significant ways: instead of universal infertility, Shelley's apocalypse is brought upon by the plague; while God plays a direct role in Grainville's text, it is only hinted at in Shelley's version through extraordinary phenomena (such as the appearance of a black sun). Where the fate of the planet and humanity are linked for Grainville, in Shelley the relation is more complex: in fact, Shelley depicts a flourishing earth in the midst of human suffering, much to the mortification of the plague-ridden inhabitants: "old and drooping as humanity had become, the world yet fresh as at creation's day" (420). The theme of Earth's endurance appears consistently through Shelley's *The Last Man*, often taking the form of bewildered, rhetorical questions:

> Why should the breeze gently stir the trees, man felt not its refreshment? Why did dark night adorn herself with stars – man saw them not? Why are there fruits, or flowers, or streams, man is not here to enjoy them? (329)

> Will the earth still keep her place among the planets; will she still journey with unmarked regularity round the sun; will the seasons change, the trees adorn themselves with leaves, and flowers shed their fragrance, in solitude? Will the mountains remain unmoved, and streams still keep a downward course towards the vast abyss; will the tides rise and fall, and the winds fan universal nature; will beasts pasture, birds fly, and fishes swim, when man, the lord, possessor, perceiver, and recorder of all these things, has passed away, as though he had never been? (413)

The repeated questions arise from the disbelief that nature could endure without a anthropocentric teleology. The questions symptomize the jealousy of a disappointed species that fails to find its own demise written into every aspect of the external world. Lionel lingers on aspects of nature in transformation – the stirring leaves, the changing seasons, the ebb and flow of the tide – resentfully imagining cycles of decay and renewal that have been lost to humanity.

Borne upon miasmic winds and the effluvium rising from the soil, the pestilence is a product of the environment. As Anne McWhir (2002: 23) observes, Shelley's representation of the plague arose from her belief in anti-contagionism, "which located the source of disease in a quality of the air itself, often a 'miasma' generated in particular but remote places and carried on the winds." The anti-contagion view displaces the human vectors of dissemination with an environment that capriciously poisons its human inhabitants. While the text remains ambiguous about the agency of the earth and the origins of the plague, critics have said a great deal about the symbolism of the disease. For

McWhir the plague is a "mixture of ideology and biology" and carried by words: "Textuality is itself potential infection, a terrifying influence" (33, 34–5). Barbara Johnson (1993: 264) argues that the "lethal universality" of the plague constitutes "a nightmarish version of the desire to establish a universal discourse, to spread equality and fraternity throughout the world." Both McWhir and Johnson find the plague implicated in the ideological and semiotic systems of humans but fail to register the significance of the plague's continuity with the earth itself.[15] As I will go on to argue, these interpretations of the plague as symbolic of an aspect of human experience follows the grain of Lionel's problematic narration, which constantly imbues both the Earth and the plague with human characteristics that it does not possess.

Even as Lionel remarks that the Earth's "fertility was a mockery" to the desolated human species, he, like the narrator of Grainville's text, cannot resist projecting older age onto the planet: "The world had grown old, and all its inmates partook of the decrepitude" (318). Even if we read Lionel's use of "the world" as a synonym for "humans," it carries the literal signification of "the world" as planet. This slippage is significant because, though the text repeatedly asserts the disconnect between the proliferating natural world and the declining human species, Lionel reverts to imagining the world as enmeshed in the same senescent proximity to extinction. In fact, Lionel's comment unfairly makes the planet's great age the cause of humanity's old age – Earth's "decrepitude" is something in which all humans "partook" in Dipesh Chakrabarty suggests that this slippage – between "world" as sum of humans and as planet – is symptomatic of a larger tendency to conflate human scales of time with planetary ones. "The global," Chakrabarty writes (2019: 24), "refers to matters that happen within human horizons of time, the multiple horizons of existential, intergenerational, and historical time," while the planetary "operate on various time tables, some compatible with human times, others vastly larger than what is involved in human calculation." To unreflectively project human scales of experience onto the planet creates a category error whereby human ethics, morality, values, and politics are made to signify for a planetary system "that not only out-scales the human but also ... has nothing moral or ethical or normative about it" (28). Thus, while referring to the planet as old might accord with the perspective of a human's short lifespan, it also imports an array of problematic ideological assumptions about the condition of the planet: the very notion of "old" does not signify at the planetary level, and only serves the anthropocentric purpose of

---

[15] Even James McKusick's (2010: 108) ecocritical reading of *The Last Man* situates the plague in an anthropocentric frame of reference by interpreting it as punishment for human sins: "there is a distinct cause-and-effect relationship between the terrible conditions of warfare and the development of a virulent strain of disease that can wipe out entire populations."

placing the earth in a sympathetic (in the case of Grainville) or antipathetic (in the case of Shelley) relation to human decline.

After claiming that "The world had grown old, and all its inmates partook of the decrepitude," Lionel continues by reflecting on the absurdity of the hierarchies that mark out human life stages:

> Why talk of infancy, manhood, and old age? We all stood equal sharers of the last throes of time-worn nature. Arrived at the same point of the world's age – there was no difference in us; the name of parent and child had lost their meaning; young boys and girls were level now with men. This was all true; but it was not less agonizing to take the admonition home. (318)

In the twilight of the human species the temporal distinctions that categorize life no longer signify. The only meaningful status is life itself: to simply survive captures the full extent of human ambition. The winnowing of humanity reveals that the chauvinist distinctions around age and gender – such as that temporal gap between the parent and child or the gulf in authority between a girl and a man – are not natural relations but culturally constructed and contingent. The crisis of extinction reveals such temporal narratives of progress – from infancy, manhood, to older age – have, from the very beginning, been used to rationalize the authority of those already in power. As Lionel exemplifies, humans also project life stages onto the planet itself – described by Lionel as "the last throes of time-worn nature" – rationalizing human sovereignty over the planet by framing it as an exhausted 'elder' in need of care. Yet Shelley's *The Last Man* reveals the dissolution of life stages as the population dwindles, and by doing so underlines the meaningless projection of senescence onto the planet as a rhetorical justification of human exploitation.

Through war, plague, and extinction, Shelley's novel represents the gradual loosening of the anthropocentric norms that center humanity while situating the earth as a supportive and nurturing supplement. As the novel progresses, humans lose faith in their own exceptionality while nature proliferates amid the ruins of once-great cities. The characters continually attempt to grapple back human sovereignty through the rhetoric of future generations. As in Grainville's narrative, the horror of extinction arises not from the unfathomable loss of life but the closing down of a human future. Lionel writes, "we call ourselves lords of the creation, wielders of the elements, masters of life and death, and we allege in excuse of this arrogance, that though the individual is destroyed, man continues for ever" (230). He continues: "we glory in the continuity of our species, and learn to regard death without terror. But when any whole nation becomes the victim of the destructive powers of exterior agents, then indeed man shrinks into insignificance, he feels his tenure of life insecure, his inheritance on earth cut off" (230). Without the promise of futurity, the scale of human time narrows to the ephemeral present: "We became ephemera, to whom the interval between the rising and setting sun was as a long drawn year of common time. We should never see our children ripen into maturity ... but we had them now – they lived, and we lived – what more could we desire?" (274). Yet when the scaffold of human generations collapses, the collective turn toward the present offers vibrant possibilities of sympathetic identification: "I know not how to express or communicate the sense of concentrated, intense, though evanescent transport, that imparadized us in the present hour. Our joys were dearer because we saw their end; they were keener because we felt, to its fullest extent, their value; they were purer because their essence was sympathy" (274). Knitting themselves together through the amplified intensity of imminent extinction, the human collective operates according to a different kind of social contract that privileges receptiveness and sympathy as ways of dwelling with others.

For both Grainville's and Shelley's last-man narratives, the precarity of human generations stimulates the imagination of a different future by annihilating it. But where Grainville's future dissipates into the ecstatic horizon of eternity (and thus the end of time), Shelley's Earth endures, revealing the asynchrony between human and planetary timescales. Lionel teases the reader with a Romantic image of an apocalyptic natural world and overturns this with the reality of a pleasant and bounteous spring:

> Feel you not the earth quake and open with agonizing groans, while the air is pregnant with shrieks and wailings, – all announcing the last days of man? No! none of these things accompanied our fall! The balmy air of spring, breathed from nature's ambrosial home, invested the lovely earth, which wakened as a young mother about to lead forth in pride her beauteous offspring to meet their sire who had been long absent. The buds decked the trees, the flowers adorned the land: the dark branches, swollen with seasonable juices, expanded into leaves, and the variegated foliage of spring, bending and singing in the breeze, rejoiced in the genial warmth of the unclouded empyrean: the brooks flowed murmuring, the sea was waveless, and the promontories that over-hung it were reflected in the placid waters. (315)

Even as Lionel underlines the dissonance that arises from the contrasting fortunes of humanity and nature, implying a painful separation of two systems that were once in sympathy, he remains tethered to anthropocentric tropes. He draws upon the discourse of reproduction: his imagination of the angry earth as "pregnant with shrieks and wailings" and the happy one as "a young mother" occurs against the backdrop of budding, swelling, warmth, and juices. The earth gains in fecundity as the human species loses the ability to reproduce. While jealousy oozes from his rhetoric, Lionel does not understand this shift in reproductive capacity to be causal. He contrasts the world to the human species to create pathos rather than suggest the more disturbing link between depopulation and unprecedented natural profusion.

The Senescence of an Ending

Both Grainville's and Shelley's dystopian narratives pivot on the relationship between human populations and the world they inhabit: the "progress" of human society strains the resources of the planet, creating the environmental conditions that result in extinction. To enhance the demographic horror, both authors alloy their discourse on populations with that of age. They link the figurative "age" of the human species to the global quantity of population rather than metrics such as average age or life expectancy. As the population dwindles, the human species becomes senescent: vulnerable, near death, non-reproductive. In addition, both authors go a step further in projecting anthropocentric age stages onto the planet: where Grainville's Earth ages alongside its declining human population, Shelley's reverts to a youthful springtime. These last-man narratives attest to a new, profoundly disturbing interrelation between population, age, and the environment in the early nineteenth century inspired by the confluence of multiple historical events: the French Revolution inspired fear of an unreflective and bloody over-turning of the "old" order; Malthus's *Essay* warned of dangerously reproductive populations; the environmental impacts of industrialization and urban overpopulation were becoming shockingly visible in polluted waterways and streets. The last-man narratives were among the first to process these vast social transformations through the lens of age. The apocalyptic intensity that arises from the confrontation of the demographic imagination with an environmental conscious-ness is made legible through the mediation of senescence.

Scholars must take a critical approach to the relation between older age and the environment to avoid perpetuating the stereotypes of older people as uncaring agents of planetary destruction or frail and hapless victims of circumstance. We must ask, moreover, how the projection of metaphors drawn from human aging affect our understanding of the planet as senescent, near death, vulnerable, and in need of care. Unlike discourse about the Anthropocene, which anchors its claims about human intervention in the materiality of the geologic record, the bodies of older people serve as a proxy surface that registers geological and environmental depredation. Our idiomatic expressions of older age capture this connection to the earth: the weathered or crannied face, the ploughed forehead, the decaying body, "old as the hills." The last-man narratives by Grainville and Shelley reveal, that since the early nineteenth century, deeply engrained beliefs about older age as decline developed alongside the accretion of anthropogenic despoilment. The imaginative linking of these two processes of decline has made registering anything but a youth-centric approach to the environment a challenge.

The following sections show how decentering youth results in a widening of intergenerational scale that not only directs our attention to a renewed sense of present possibility, but also demonstrates the potential for imagining queer, Indigenous, and senescent futures. I turn now to P. D. James's *The Children of Men*, a sterility dystopia published 166 years after Shelley's *The Last Man*. What explains the return to the genre of demographic and reproductive horror? The concerns that inspired Grainville and Shelley – fears about destructive progress and growing populations, of human and planetary senescence – never disappeared, though capitalism developed ideological mystifications to obscure these anxieties. In the late twentieth century, however, the accumulated effects of extractive capitalism became reified into holes in the ozone, islands of plastic waste in the sea, rising temperatures, and unprecedented volatile weather. The discourse of populations takes on a renewed Malthusian urgency in the context of ballooning carbon footprints and the economic burdens of an aging population in Western nations. We have returned, in other words, to the concerns that animated the last-man narratives of the early nineteenth century, where the aging of the individual was used to imaginatively mediate between the temporality of the human species and the planet. But where Grainville and Shelley represent this as an existential problem, more recent novelists show how the apportioning of this diminishing, precarious future accords with the politics of sexuality and race.

Queer Genre/ations

Lord, thou hast been our refuge: from one generation to another. Before the mountains were brought forth, or ever the earth and the world were made: thou art God from everlasting, and world without end. Thou turnest man to destruction: again thou sayest, Come again, ye children of men. For a thousand years in thy sight are but as yesterday: seeing that is past as a watch in the night.

    "Psalm 90," *The Book of Common Prayer*

In addition to providing the title for *The Children of Men*, Psalm 90 appears late in the novel as Theo presides over an improvised funeral for Luke, the man who fathered the first child in twenty-seven years. The rest of the group listen in silence: Julian, the woman carrying the unborn child; Rolf, her cuckolded husband, who watches in bitter silence; and Miriam, a midwife. The passage solemnizes the occasion while underlining the dangers that threaten the group – the Warden of England, Xan Lypiatt, who searches after the group that have challenged his dictatorial regime; Julian's brooding husband, Rolf, who will avenge himself by informing the government; time itself, with the doubled anxiety of Julian's imminent labor and the menace of impending extinction. The passage draws attention to the sense of relief of generational passage, which apotheosizes to the religious sense of "refuge" – that even in the midst of destruction, the thought that another generation to come, the "children of men," inspires hope for a better future. Yet this comfort is framed by the temporal expansiveness of God and the "world without end" – the ongoingness of a world that persists regardless of human extinction, the deepness of a time, where "a thousand years in thy sight are but as yesterday," that shames human vanity. Generational assurance for the future, that is, exists in an uncomfortable relation to generational precarity and contingency.

In one of the few scholarly articles to reflect on the relation between age studies and ecocriticism, Kathleen Woodward (2020: 54) proposes "generational time" as an imaginative stimulus for reckoning with the temporal scale of the climate crisis, which extends far beyond the scope of the singular life. She writes that generational time might "press home the urgency presented by climate change" by "involve[ing] us affectively as well as cognitively. Entailing two, three, and four generations, perhaps even more, generational time is our singular way of understanding future time, linking us in altogether meaningful ways to others whose futures we care about deeply" (54). Citing the neoliberal breakdown of "values that bind people together in meaningful and intimate ways," Woodward believes that the filiative timescale of generations provides a model for the kind of intersubjectivity needed to confront the climate crisis (46). In what follows I argue that generational time is a deeply problematic solution – one that depends on heteronormative ideals that restrict, rather than expand, the collective effort; that reproduce, rather than resist, the neoliberal milieu that underwrites anthropogenic climate change. Where Woodward grapples with a precarious future by proposing the assurance of generational links, I suggest confronting such precarity with the contingency that arises from a queer sense of intergenerational time.

Future generations, often sentimentalized in the figure of the child, play a major role in environmental discourse as a catalyzing argument for climate activism: for future generations to survive, we need to ensure that the planet is inhabitable in the future. In *No Future*, however, Lee Edelman (2004: 2) argues against what he calls "reproductive futurity" – a heteronormative orientation toward the future that closes down the possibility of queer life. For Edelman, reproductive futurity is symbolically registered by the naturalized goodness of the child, for whose sake almost any sacrifice in the present can be rationalized:

"we are no more able to conceive of a politics without a fantasy of the future than we are able to conceive of a future without the figure of the Child. That figural Child alone embodies the citizen as an ideal, entitled to claim full rights to its future share in the nation's good, though always at the cost of limiting the rights 'real' citizens are allowed" (11). *The Children of Men* attracts Edelman's fleeting derision as a text that distills the most heinous aspects of reproductive futurism: "If, however, there is *no baby* and, in consequence, *no future*, then the blame must fall on the fatal lure of sterile, narcissistic enjoyments understood as inherently destructive of meaning and therefore as responsible for the undoing of social organization, collective reality, and, inevitably, life itself" (13). For Edelman, *The Children of Men* trivializes forms of queer sexuality: as the narrator observes in the novel, "Sex totally divorced from procreation has become almost meaninglessly acrobatic" (James [1992] 2018: 164). The impulse to secure a future for human generations requires confronting the heteronormative impulse that degrades queer life (and the concomitant degradation of all forms of non-human life).[16]

For Nicole Seymour (2013: 6), Edelman's anti-social thesis "leave[s] the health and future of the planet looking like a frivolous concern." Rebekah Sheldon (2016: 161), however, in her Edelman-inspired reading of Alfonso Cuarón's film adaptation of *The Children of Men*, suggests that the sterility dystopia presents a morbid *solution* to the problem of environmental crisis: "Against the background threat of uncontrolled proliferation, infertility appears as the antidote for, rather than the symbol of, climate change and its upending of rational management." Ecocritics such as Catriona Sandilands (2014: 310) have used Edelman's thesis to reframe some of the central assumptions of environmental activism:

> Why is the future Child the privileged figure around whom environmental ethics and politics are organized, and what about the children – and former children – who might well argue that nothing has ever been saved in their names? ... if the future is understood to reside in the welfare of beings too young to care for themselves, then what kinds of political practice are we agreeing to in order to secure that particular future in the face of a complex present that happens to be full of wildly diverse Others?

---

[16] For Alison Kafer (2013: 31), Edelman's argument about queers applies to disabled people as well: "children serve as the sign of the future; the kind of future that awaits us will be determined by the kind of children we bear. Illness, 'defect,' 'deviance,' and disability are positioned as fundamentally damaging to the fabric of the community ... To put it bluntly, disabled people were – and often are – figured as threats to futurity." In the way it knits economic non-productivity with biological non-re-productivity, Kafer's expansion of Edelman's thesis provides a useful starting point for drawing out the senescent implications of *no future*: "some populations are already marked as having no future, as destined for decay, as always already disabled" (Kafer 34).

Both Sandilands and Seymour offer queer alternatives to reproductive futurity that do not entail writing off modes of care for future generations, "in which generativity is not reduced to reproductivity, in which the future is not limited to a repetition of a heteronormative ideal of the Same" (Sandilands 2014: 315).[17]

While ecocritics have used Edelman's *No Future* to queer the future orientation of environmental redemption, the age studies scholar Cynthia Port (2012: 3) has used his thesis to ask similarly urgent questions regarding older age. She aligns older people and queers in the cultural imagination through shared non-reproductivity: both are "outside mainstream temporalities and standing in the way of, rather than contributing to, the promise of the future." "Like other minorities," she writes, "the elderly often find themselves 'outside the rational time of capital, nation, and family' and therefore without a comfortable place in chrononormative structures and institutions" (5). Port, like the queer ecologists I cite above, argues for attending to the complexity and richness of present experience – for reckoning with a model of generativity that is horizontal as well as vertical, for drawing out the thick relations that situate an individual within a particular time and place. Sarah Falcus (2020: 72) builds upon the work of Edelman and Port in her age studies inspired reading of *The Children of Men*, a novel that, in her reading, represents the demographic dread that arises from a world populated with older people: the threat "of no children and the end of the species – is inextricably linked to and metonymically represented by the threat of ageing itself and the burden of an ageing population." While I agree with Falcus, my work in this section – and, indeed, across the Element as a whole – suggests that the sterility dystopia does more than symptomatize the fears of an aging population. I understand the genre as a response to the eco-demographic problems of the Anthropocene: a collection of experiments that reimagine and renegotiate the sympathetic and epistemological gaps between human and planetary timescales.[18]

Age plays a central role in both medical discourse and popular representations of women's fertility. Doctors refer to a pregnancy as "geriatric" if a woman

---

[17] See also Seymour (2013: 18–19): "What if we could imagine that environmental catastrophe *does* matter, even, or perhaps especially, if we are not going to witness its effects? . . . I argue that a concept of queer time that is attuned to environmentalism's focus on futurity – on the long- and short-term effects of policies and products; on health outcomes for humans and non-humans alike; on sustainable practices – is one place to start." Bruce Erickson (2010: 324) also provides a thoughtful approach, suggesting that: "thinking through a politics of nature without a future means rethinking nature such that it is not bent toward the utility of power. Opening ourselves to the possibilities of history means addressing the ways in which the ideologies and concrete practices that have formed out of current understandings of nature represent more about the desired human outcomes than they do about anything nonhuman."

[18] As I note in the introduction, the generational short-circuiting of the sterility dystopia should provoke us to critique the larger cultural and social implications of youth-centered arguments for environmental preservation.

is over age thirty-five. Family members often remind women of their ticking "biological clock" to add a sense of urgency to conception. As yet another example of what Susan Sontag (1972: 38) describes as the "double standard about aging," while growing older plays an important role in the fertility of men, it is more likely to form one variable among many, alongside factors such as chronic health conditions, obesity, drug use, and exposure to toxins. Thus, older age has a particular force for women, as it underlines the temporal contingency involved with the reproductive body that will eventually age beyond the capacity to produce new offspring.[19] Eve Sedgwick (2003: 147) asks us to consider the temporality of reproductive contingency as a challenge to the "generational narrative that's characterized by a distinctly Oedipal regularity and repetitiveness." She uses intergenerational friendship to model a relational mode that helps us to imagine the startling possibility that "the future may be different from the present" (146):[20]

> On this scene, an older person doesn't love a younger as someone who will someday be where she now is, or vice versa. No one is, so to speak, passing on the family name; there's a sense in which our life narratives will barely overlap. There's another sense in which they slide up more intimately alongside one another than can any lives that are moving forward according to the regular schedule of the generations. It is one another immediately, one another as the present fullness of a becoming whose arc may extend no further, whom we each must learn best to apprehend, fulfill, and bear company. (149)

Sedgwick's queer affiliation helps to draw together ecocritical and age studies approaches to the problem of reproductive futurity. First, she does not locate older age in a hierarchy above or below youth but enmeshed together in the present. This resists the heteronormative ideal that privileges one stage of life – whether it be the child or the reproductive years of the human lifespan – while ghettoizing the later years as non-productive excess. Second, in embracing the "present fullness of becoming whose arc may extend no further," Sedgwick connects the contingency of the lifespan to uncertainty and hope in the future. To acknowledge that the present might be all that we have does not impoverish our approach to future – of the planet, of our lives in older age – but provides the

---

[19] The *Dobbs* ruling by the US Supreme Court, removing the right to abortion, serves as a shocking reminder of right-wing attempts to control the reproduction of women. While reproductive futurity is deeply entrenched in the cultural unconscious, it is important to acknowledge how this ideal has been constructed through the fraught politics over women's bodies and that heterosexuality does not necessarily entail reproduction.

[20] Judith Halberstam (2005: 5) writes that an important element of heteronormative temporality is "the time of inheritance": this "refers to an overview of generational time within which values, wealth, goods, and morals are passed through family ties from one generation to the next. It also connects the family to the historical past of the nation, and glances ahead to connect the family to the future of both familial and national stability."

profoundly liberating opportunity to think outside the generational lockstep that perpetually defers the necessity for action (on climate change, for example) into an ever-receding future.

This concept of queer intergenerational futurity – a future that is not assured but hoped for, necessarily different from the past and present in surprising and sometimes disconcerting ways – must compete with the pervasive belief that human life would be meaningless without future generations. In *Why Worry About Future Generations?*, the philosopher Samuel Scheffler (2018: 42–3) turns to *The Children of Men* to exemplify his argument that

> most of us would find the prospect of humanity's imminent extinction unbearably depressing. Faced with this impending catastrophe, our lives would be suffused with grief and gloom. And the effects on us would extend beyond the realm of the emotions; the point is not just that we would feel sad or unhappy or sorrowful. At least as significant is the fact that many of the activities that we had previously regarded as worthwhile would no longer seem to us as appealing.

But the work of Edelman and Sedgwick demonstrates that a renewed engagement with the present does not close down future possibility but disclose it: that the very possibility of a meaningful and different future arises from the intimacy of immediate experience rather than borrowing meaning from a state of affairs that does not yet exist. An obsessive, heteronormative compulsion toward the future, the belief that future generations are a necessary condition for existential significance, results in a present that is out of sync with itself.

Instead, we might take a temporally neutral attitude. Building upon the work of Derek Parfit, Helen Small (2010: 150) observes that "the remoteness of our own old age while we are young opens the way for caring less about age, but if we were to consider our temporal location within our expected lifespan 'neutrally,' Parfit suggests, we should put ourselves in the way of a much happier old age." According to Parfit, most of us demonstrate a temporal bias toward the near; for example, we would prefer to experience a small pleasure in the future than have experienced a large pleasure in the past. Temporal neutrality, however, suggests that the rational approach is to consider all pleasures and pains on the same temporal plane – the larger good, in this case, is more desirable than the smaller regardless of where it falls in relation to the present. The pleasure of smoking a cigarette while young must be reckoned in relation to the damage it will cause to the older person the youth will one day become. Commuting to work in a gas-guzzling truck must be weighed in relation to rising sea levels and temperatures, however remote these environmental consequences might seem. Both our aging and carbon footprint are shaped by a bias toward the near, which obscures the potentially devastating future consequences of small pleasures in the present.

Temporal neutrality helps to enlarge the scope of Sedgwick's argument about queer intergenerationality by providing her deeply synchronic model with a diachronic thrust. "It is one another immediately, one another as the present fullness of a becoming whose arc may extend no further," Sedgwick writes (2003: 149), privileging an immediacy of the present. In pushing against the lockstep of generational progression, Sedgwick's model risks reproducing the bias toward the near and immediate that has resulted in harmful behaviors to the environment and our aging. Temporal neutrality challenges us to cultivate an extended, durable immediacy that spills over into the past and future. While such an ecstatic perspective might strain the imagination, it also might be the only way to confront the twinned temporal prejudices that posit a devastating disconnect between myself now and the older person I might become, my consumption habits now and their effect on the climate in the future. Considered through the lens of temporal neutrality – where past, present, and future exist on the same ethical plane – Sedgwick's model of queer immediacy can serve as a reparative approach to remote events such as climate change and aging. As an alternative to the receding future of generational thinking, Sedgwick's immediacy must extend beyond the now to cultivate an equally intimate relation to the future. This shift of perspective counters an unreflective belief in "passing the torch" which has, through the prospect of endless accumulation and generational futurity, set the world on fire.

As I have argued so far, the temporal scale of climate change can be made legible by anchoring it in the intimate experience of our own aging and our affective relationship to others aging alongside us. But we need a model that goes beyond generational time, which carries problematic heteronormative assumptions. Linking queer intergenerationality with temporal neutrality pushes the affective immediacy of the now into the ethical judgements that we make about the future. Instead of Edelman's *no future*, I propose abolishing – or aspiring to grapple across – the temporal and imaginative gap that separates the present from the future. Rather than perennially defer to future generations, we must be made to dwell in the future: a future charged with both the banal reality of the everyday and the thrilling sensation of an embodied present. The privileged genre for this kind of temporal recalibration is surely science fiction, which draws an imagined possibility (oftentimes an imagined future) into the realm of the reader's present experience. In what follows, I focus on the role of genre in providing a set of formal coordinates that allow for the mapping of age onto the planetary timescale. Placing the generational short-circuiting of *The Children of Men* within this larger generic context suggests that the novel, far from merely sentimentalizing heterosexual reproduction, instead provokes a queer confrontation with the troubling politics of demographic change.

Science fiction has a kind of dubious privilege when it comes to environmental literature and climate change. Amitav Ghosh (2016: 27) writes that the generic gatekeeping that assigns prestige to the realist novel must be reconfigured in the wake of climatic events that normalize the improbable. The gap that once separated science fiction from the 'real' has closed: it no longer represents an escape from our current milieu but a compelling representation of events that are "actually happening on this earth, at this time."[21] Timothy Clark (2019: 99) avers, writing that the Anthropocene "may find its analogue in modes of the fantastic, new forms of magic realism, or texts in which old distinctions between 'character' and 'environment' become fragile or break down." For Stephanie LeMenager (2017: 222), the climate crisis causes a "struggle for genre," a phrase that captures the attempt to "to find new patterns of expectation and new means of living with an unprecedented set of limiting conditions." Writing in the midst of environmental crisis has inspired a reckoning with genre that challenges our expectations about what counts as "serious" literature (a perennial bugbear in science fiction scholarship) by recalibrating the limits of realist probability and "everyday" catastrophe.

This generic disruption often takes on a generational resonance in narratives where the assurance of the future can no longer be taken for granted, where new and old orders conflict, or where the unpredictable and improbable are placed within the realm of reasonable expectation. Though most theorists of science fiction acknowledge that the genre is "an inherently, and radically, future-oriented process," the specific form of generationality that underwrites this future orientation has not received much scrutiny from critics (Csiscery-Ronay 2008: 3). For Darko Suvin (1979: 84), science fiction allows for the escape from "constrictive old norms into a different and alternative timestream": it is a "device for historical estrangement." Carl Freedman (2000: 55) emphasizes that "The future is crucial to science fiction not as a specific chronological register, but as a locus of radical *alterity* to the mundane status quo, which is thus estranged and historicized as the concrete past of a potential future." In its temporal displacements and estrangements, there is a queer sense of generational succession at work in science fiction. On the one hand, the future contains an alterity that distinguishes it from the heteronormative reproduction of the now, breaking the bleak cycle of repetition

---

[21] It is worth noting that some readers of *The Great Derangement* have criticized Ghosh of perpetuating generic gatekeeping. Ursula Heise (2018), for example, finds his devaluing of science fiction as a genre of climate change to be unnecessary: science fiction novels, she writes, "have explored the upheavals and catastrophes climate change will bring, but also and above all the altered everyday experiences and psychological structures it will generate."

that Eve Sedgwick (2003: 147) describes as: "it happened to my father's father, it happened to my father, it is happening to me, it will happen to my son, and it will happen to my son's son." And yet this future bears the traces of its estrangement from the present and must be understood as linked to this present in its very difference. There is, in other words, a queer blending of tense in science fiction that provokes an awareness of the synchronic and simultaneous in the midst of diachronic succession.

The sterility dystopia puts the diachronic axis of generational temporality and the synchronic axis of intergenerational temporality into crisis. In *The Children of Men*, Theo muses that

> We can experience nothing but the present moment, live in no other second of time, and to understand this is as close as we can get to eternal life. But our minds reach back through centuries for the reassurance of our ancestry and, without the hope of posterity, for our race if not for ourselves, without the assurance that we being dead yet live, all pleasures of the mind and senses sometimes seem to me no more than pathetic and crumbling defences shored up against our ruin. (13)

The fullness of the present intersects with the assurances of the past and future, finds comfort in its position between two certainties. Removing the possibility of future generations destroys the fantasy of a personal existence beyond the limitations of the human lifespan. For critics such as Edelman and Scheffler, who gesture to passages like this one to support their opposed arguments about the value of future generations, James's novel suggests that belief in the continuation of the human race is necessary to confer meaning on our actions in the present. Theo's account focuses on the individual, whose instinct for self-preservation finds consolation in the knowledge that his or her legacy (whether directly in the form of children or indirectly through the effects on future generations) will be carried forward in time.

Yet the novel goes on to develop a more nuanced account of generations by linking them to other forms of affiliation (as opposed to filiation) across time. The progression of academic generations serves as one alternative. As an Oxford professor, Theo begins his career as the favorite student of the curmudgeonly Jasper, who would select "an undergraduate, invariably male, for his approval and patronage" (61). Theo wonders if "this wasn't [Jasper's] way of confronting age, time, the inevitable blunting of the mind's keen edge, his personal illusion of immortality" (63). The generational logic that underwrites the sense of immortality (I will be part of the generations to come) is coded deeply into the social fabric that knits individuals together. But this is based on a very fragile sense of responsibility, which Theo rejects when his former mentor requests to move into

Theo's large, five-bedroom house: "It looked as if the thirty-year-old bill for benefits received, the special coaching, the expensive dinners, the theatre and opera tickets, is belatedly being presented. But the thought of sharing St John Street, of the violation of privacy, of my increasing responsibility for a difficult old man, repels me. I owe Jasper a great deal, but I don't owe him that" (68). The relation between Theo and his mentor demonstrates, through its arbitrary, misogynist origins and the ease with which it is shrugged off, the fragility of all generational links – even those of blood – that persist through time. The depopulating conceit of the sterility dystopia reveals that the assurance of futurity that generational time offers is not a given, but something that requires work to nurture.

In addition to children and academic mentorship, the novel explores generational responsibility at the planetary scale. Carl Inglebach, a member of the ruling council beneath Xan, argues that universal infertility has marked "the end of our care for the physical world and our planet. What does it matter what turds we leave behind as legacies of our brief disruptive tenancy?" (139–40). What point in acting as steward of the planet when there will be no humans alive in the future to enjoy it? Through the lack of future generations, Inglebach justifies the excremental practices of late capitalism that view the planet as a resource to be exploited instead of sustained. His view is echoed by other characters in the novel who anticipate planetary death: "you can't mourn for unborn grandchildren when there never was a hope of them. This planet is doomed anyway"; "It was a generation programmed for failure"; "They live without hope on a dying planet"; "he could almost smell the accumulated rubbish of the dead years" (63, 78, 84, 182). While the characters might rhetorically position the infertility crisis as cause for existential and environmental despair, there is reason to invert the cause-and-effect relationship. The lack of future generations rationalizes the kind of extractive practices that were already in place before the "Omega" event that sterilized the human population. Sterility is the symptom, not the cause. The disease begins with the neoliberal breakdown of social responsibility, relationality, and an ethics of care for the planet, exemplified in Theo's confession that "I don't want anyone to look to me, not for protection, not for happiness, not for love, not for anything" (37). The lack of future generations merely writes large the inability to construct meaningful relations in the present, which has already been liquidated of the care and connectedness that make the project of preservation possible and worthwhile.[22] This emptied out present reveals the bad faith of the discourse about future generations, which is instrumentalized to sustain

---

[22] In *Old Futures: Speculative Fiction and Queer Possibility*, Alexis Lothian (2018: 90) suggests that "James frames the end of reproduction as a direct result of a moral failure to engage with the future." But, as I argue here, the failure arises from an attention overly attuned to the future, which has resulted in an impoverished relation to the present.

the practices of extractive capitalism (and "the turds [it] leaves behind") that nullify the very existence of the futurity it sentimentalizes.[23]

The Children of Men gestures to the *longue durée* of the infertility crisis through Theo's academic specialization in nineteenth-century History, which recalls both the thematic concerns of the last-man narratives I analyze above and the origins of the capitalist practices that culminate in human extinction. Though "History," the narrator sardonically notes, "is the least rewarding discipline for a dying species," it is still essential to understand how the characters position themselves in relation to the crisis (16).[24] Theo remembers the paintings that his mother would produce from old prints of Victorian scenes, "a crowded railway terminus with bonneted women seeing off their men to the Crimean War; a Victorian family, the women in furs and bustles, decorating the church for Christmas; Queen Victoria escorted by her consort, surrounded by crinolined children, opening the Great Exhibition" (33). For a novel so invested in the social and cultural upheavals of an aging population, the nineteenth century provides a resonant touchstone. As I argued in the previous section, the nineteenth century alloyed an optimistic belief in human progress with acute demographic anxieties: from the New Poor Law of 1834, which funneled large numbers of impoverished older people into humiliating conditions in the workhouse, to heated debates about the fairness of universal older age pensions in the 1890s, nineteenth-century institutions helped to shape modern attitudes toward aging as a social problem. Theo views the Victorian age "through a telescope at once so close and yet infinitely remote, fascinating in its energy, its moral seriousness, its brilliance and squalor" (33). History, in other words, does not merely offer a nostalgic escape into the past, but a way of telescoping that past into the present. In a world increasingly populated by older people, the turn to History – written in the aging bodies of the populace and the pages of Theo's books – provides a new means of encounter with an impoverished and futureless Now.

While he examines postcards in the Pitt Rivers Museum in Oxford, Theo encounters a replica of a photograph "of the founding fathers of this secular cathedral to Victorian confidence, John Ruskin and Sir Henry Ackland sitting together in 1874" (151). "Here was Victorian confidence, Victorian earnestness,"

---

23 Brian Aldiss's ([1964] 2011: 125) *Greybeard*, a spiritual predecessor to James's 1992 sterility dystopia, frames the desire for future generations explicitly in terms of consumerism: "The democracies – and our friends in the Communist community – need a new generation, however come by, to work in their assembly lines and consume their goods . . . Hence this stinking war, as we quarrel over what's left. . . . Let's have a toast – to the future generation of consumers, however many heads or assholes they have!" (125).

24 Interestingly, Theo's work in History serves as one of the reasons her is chosen to help Julian: "But two of us, Luke and I, have read some of your books" Julian says. And Theo drily responds: "It's unwise to judge an academic's personal probity from his written work" (James [1992] 2018: 59).

Theo reflects, "the respect for learning, for craftsmanship, for art; the conviction that the whole of man's life could be lived in harmony with the natural world" (151). There is no room for the Victorian confidence toward improvement in the barren twenty-first century. Most importantly, the twenty-first century leaves behind the conviction that "man's life could be lived in harmony with the natural world." Theo's account, of course, ignores how the Victorians dotted the horizon with coal burning chimneys and populated their factories with alienated labor. As Nathan Hensley and Philip Steer write (2019: 2–3),

> The nineteenth century therefore stands as the origin of not just the irreversible ecological degradation we have inherited from our nineteenth-century forebears, but also the global interconnection and vast asymmetries of power that are the legacies of the British Empire in the present.... The uncanny but perversely material presence of the Victorian era's coal-fired and imperial past, then, means that our new contemporary is best viewed as but a moment in a much longer unfolding.

A false hope arises from the projection of nostalgia backwards and forwards in time: desire for a past that did not exist – for a nineteenth century in "harmony with the natural world" – provides a tenuous ground for hope in a human future that will not and cannot exist. This alienation from the real conditions of existence writes large the mystifications that makes heteronormative generational thinking possible: misremembering and idealizing the past allows for the rationalization of unsustainable practices in the fantasy of progress without end.

In its use of the fantastic and improbable, the genre of science fiction might be viewed as mystifying the narrative of inexorable modern progress. And while many instances of the genre exemplify a technophilic tendency, the sterility dystopia demonstrates the genre's radical potential by linking futurity to queer modes of social organization. The birth that concludes *The Children of Men* is not an appalling retreat to reproductive futurity (as Edelman believes), but an exemplary, because failed, opportunity for imagining social connection across the attenuated links of blood and generations. Though characterized by his reluctance to embrace obligation, a reluctance registered most powerfully by the accidental murder of his own child while reversing out of his driveway, Theo nevertheless sparks into a sense of connectedness when he feels the heartbeat of the unborn child: "That moment when he had knelt at Julian's feet, had felt her child move under his hand, had bound him to them irrevocably" (225). In its decoupling of the child from the biological father, the novel makes the first small step toward opening the possibility of queer forms of social cohesion that break the generational lockstep that perpetuates the destructive practices of the past into the future. Donna Haraway (2016a: 102–3) pushes against generational logic with her use of the term "kin": "the stretch and recomposition of kin are allowed by the fact that all earthlings are kin in the deepest sense, and it is past time to practice better care of kinds-as-assemblages (not species one at a time). Kin is an assembling sort of word.... Ancestors turn out to be very interesting strangers; kin are unfamiliar (outside what we thought was family or gens), uncanny, haunting, active." *The Children of Men* offers the tenuous possibility of a future mediated by intergenerational kinship rather than heteronormative filiation through the encounter with an unfamiliar and plural now rather than the anticipation of a predicable future.

In *Archaeologies of the Future*, Frederic Jameson (2007: 187) writes that science fiction "narrative cannot really deal with generations either, or with generational time ... All of diachronic time is compressed into this single apocalyptic instant, which the narrative relates as the memory of old people." For Jameson, apocalyptic synchronicity overcomes generational diachronicity through the form of retrospective narration, which he associates with the backward glance of older age. Connotatively associated with stasis, older age stands in for narrative's inability to register the "slow changes in historical time" (187). But older age can serve as more than a mere metaphor for retrospective narrative that has reached its formal limits. It can serve as the very means of sensitizing our attention to the *durée* of gradual and marginalized temporalities that skim just below the threshold of perception. Instead of opposing apocalyptic synchronicity and generational diachronicity through the figure of older age, thinking in the terms of intergenerational kinship attunes us to the way these temporal modes overlap with one another. In this view, older age does not embody the exhausted, backward glance of retrospective narration, but forms one mode of attention among others – one that, through the scale provided by the long life and enmeshment within an intergenerational network in the present, is particularly attuned to the slow and gradual transformations that a cultural obsession with youth (as the embodiment of futurity) obscures.[25]

Thus, the aging and depopulating world of the sterility dystopia can be read as more than existential doom, but as foregrounding older age as a reparative form of attention based in intergenerational kinship, which manifests through an idiosyncratic attentiveness to the gradual. Closing down the possibility of future generations activates an increased investment in the granularity of the Now, which ironically creates the conditions for different, more sustainable futures: "He thought then, as he thought now, of time passing, inexorable, unforgiving, unstoppable time," Theo reflects (212). This kind of attentiveness, Rob Nixon

---

[25] In his seminal work on utopia, Ernst Bloch ([1954] 1986: 117) defines the principle of hope as inherently youthful: "All fresh strength necessarily contains this New, and moves towards it. Its best places are: youth, times which are on the point of changing, creative expression."

(2011: 2) argues, makes legible the "slow violence" of environmental devastation: "violence that occurs gradually and out of sight, a violence of delayed destruction that is dispersed across time and space, an attritional violence that is typically not viewed as violence at all." The problem with slow violence relates to representation and scale: "how can we imaginatively and strategically render visible vast force fields of interconnectedness against the attenuating effects of temporal and geographical distance?" (38). Genre functions as an interface, a way of drawing into visibility the slow effects of processes that began long before their causes have become evident.

The ability for genre to function as an interface for making slow violence visible is matched, in *The Children of Men*, by the temporality of gestation, which underwrites the narrative form of the novel. Though foreshadowed, Julian's late-term pregnancy remains a secret until chapter 21 (out of 33), approximately two-thirds of the way through the novel. The revelation inspires a tectonic shift in how temporality functions in the novel, both at the phenomenal level of subjective experience and the formal one of genre. In a world without children, Theo experiences time as "inexorable, unforgiving, unstoppable": a march into "a world with no future where, all too soon, the very words justice, compassion, society, struggle, evil, would be unheard echoes on an empty air" (212, 160). The lack of children forces Theo into an existential confrontation with the conditions that precipitated the crisis: such a painful confrontation, the novel suggests, enables a reckoning with the present on its own terms and, even in the midst of despair (or perhaps because of it), opens the possibility of change in the future. When he becomes aware of the child, however, everything snaps back to the status quo: when the child ensures future generations of the human race, the present becomes at once gloriously revitalized and surreptitiously repetitive. Awaiting the child's birth, Theo takes refuge in a present that is blissfully disconnected from time and responsibility: "the three of them could live in safety until the child was born. He could see no further and he told himself that need see no further" (295). After the birth of the child and defeat of the Warden of England, Theo puts on the ring symbolizing Xan's authoritarian power, remarking to Julian that "It's useful for the present. I shall take it off in time" (341). While I argue above that the child's vulnerability requires networks of care that open the possibility of queer, intergenerational kinship, its birth also offers the tantalizing possibility of a return to the same destructive patterns of tyranny and self-interest that gave rise to the dystopian society.

Instead of making legible slow violence, the birth of the child obscures it by making the present appear as another version of an eternal past that extends into an eternal future – the "natural" order has been restored, and the affective force of the familiar lulls Theo into a myopic, nostalgic acceptance of the status quo.

The revelation of the pregnancy, moreover, provokes a shift in the novel's generic mode: where the first two-thirds of the novel carefully trace the psychological effects of universal infertility on the individual and the degeneration of governance into authoritarianism, the final third shifts into the fast-paced plot of escape as Julian races to give birth beyond the clutches of Xan's oppressive regime. As the plot accelerates – reflected in the narrative discourse by the breathless escape in a car – the novel trades the realism of the pre-pregnancy section for the thrills of the fantastic: a rogue gang of young people who remind Theo of "painted South Sea Islanders with their top-knots" murder Luke, the father of the child (258); Theo shoots Xan through the heart in a standoff and improbably assumes the power of the state. The shift in genre captures – in its radical break with the expectations set out in the first section, through its accelerated pace and exaggerated adventure elements – a rejection of the attentiveness necessary to perceive the subtle movements that constitute slow violence. We are presented, instead, with the epiphany of the birth. The miracle exaggerates and amplifies – the reader's attention is drawn away from the underlying social causes of the crisis in favor of a celebratory return of the heteronormative social order. While one might read this as James's novel capitulating to the gravity of such norms, the very unconventionality of the generic shift – along with, in the final pages, Theo's embrace of the authoritarian powers he resisted throughout most of the novel – serves as a warning to engage in the delicate work of identifying slow violence and building intergenerational kinship. The shock of familiarity, registered through the birth of the child and the return of generational progression, snaps the characters and even the form of the text back to the conventional, uncritical, and hegemonic mode of being that obscures the slow violence of environmental collapse.

To argue that the sterility dystopia provides a means of registering slow violence might seem to go against the grain of science fiction's larger investment with futurity. Lawrence Buell (2016: 16), for example, writes that "apocalypticism is a mismatch for the 'slow violence' of how environmental deterioration actually works." Timothy Clark (2016: 21–2), referencing *The Children of Men*, argues that "In such plots the slow-motion and distributed nature of demographic effects, whether of an aging population or a preference for male progeny, take on a cartoon-like extremism, whereas the often-insidious power of demographic change actually lies in its dispersed, gradual, low-visibility, its contamination or catalytic supplementation of innumerable other questions and areas of life." But my argument suggests that the sterility dystopia provides much more than the mere spectacle of apocalypse and the escapism of magical thinking. By removing the assurance of future generations, the sterility dystopia turns temporality inward, toward the present experience of intergenerational imbrication. In his defense of science fiction as an attempt to capture the "inhumanly large and long" scale of the non-human world, Mark McGurl (2012: 541) asks, "what principle of limitation will be called upon to give that vaulting largeness and longness a meaningful form?" The sterility dystopia offers the limit case of human extinction. My reading of the genre suggests that future possibility does not depend on the birth of a new generation, but on a queer sense of intergenerational kinship in the shared now. The future depends on it.

In my turn toward questions of genre and generations, I have attempted to show that proximity to the end – whether in terms of individual mortality or ecological catastrophe – offers an opportunity to confront the problem of extinction from a perspective that resists both the sinister implications of decline ideology and the heteronormative assumptions of generational progress. The future can no longer be taken for granted – this is an aspect of our current environmental crisis that the sterility dystopia powerfully registers by removing the assurance of future generations. Older age, in this case, serves as much more than the symbolic concentrate of these doomed energies, and instead provides a model for how we might confront them. While an older person has less potential time in the future than a young one, there is nothing about this quantity of time that necessitates despair or anguish. An older person will not necessarily be more unhappy than the younger. In fact, there is a great deal to suggest that the older person might have the upper hand: through the accumulation of memories that, even if not always pleasurable, richly texture the experience of the present; through the friendship, immediate and remembered, with people across generations; through the sense of temporal scale that only the long life can provide. Though these are contingent rather than essential attributes of older age, they attest to the reparative possibility at the end of the human lifespan. When confronted with a diminishing future, the overwhelming emphasis on the child and generational progress can result in a profound despair. Older age, however, reveals that this despair is not a necessary or even likely outcome when one approaches an end.

This reading might appear to go against the grain of the sterility dystopia genre, which conjures suspense through the reader's anxiety about the imminent extinction of the human species. But in representing a depopulating and aging society, texts such as *The Children of Men* also gesture to the hermeneutic possibilities that arise from a heightened awareness of contingency and immediacy (possibilities obscured by an exclusively future orientation). As I have argued in this section, the tension that arises between older age and environmental crisis in the sterility dystopia can be used to model an affective disposition better suited to the challenges of an uncertain future. To inch closer to the end of life, to accumulate history through memory and in the fibers of one's body, does not entail closing off the circuits of care that link the older person to the future of a planet in peril.

Senescent Futurity

In the introduction to *The World, the Text, and the Critic*, Edward Said (1983: 1–5) pushes against the tendency of literary scholarship to transcendentalize texts – either treating them like a timeless aesthetic object or turning inward to the aporias of textuality – in favor of situating texts in the social realities that made them possible. Though Said's point now forms an integral part of our disciplinary unconscious, the way he rationalizes his argument through a contrast between filiation and affiliation provide a starting point for an intersectional approach to race, age, and the environment. For Said, the "filiative scheme belongs to the realms of nature and of 'life,'" whereas affiliation belongs exclusively to culture and society" (20). He identifies a pattern where late-nineteenth- and early-twentieth-century texts challenge filiation through "the failure of the capacity to produce or generate children" (16). "Childless couples, orphaned children, aborted child-births, and unregenerately celibate men and women" symptomize the multiple alienations of capitalist, urban modernity and reveal that "few things are as problematic and as universally fraught as what we might have supposed to be the mere natural continuity between one generation and the next" (17, 16). Yet as the biological relationships of filiation are denaturalized and challenged, affiliative relationships – social and cultural forms including institutions, political parties, professional organizations, and class consciousness – emerge as compensatory social bonds (17).

Though these affiliative relations rise in importance precisely because they are socially constructed instead of biological, they are nevertheless imbued with the "vestiges of the kind of authority associated in the past with filiative order": "obedience, fear, love, respect, and instinctual conflict" (19, 20). Affiliative relations, in other words, take on the affective force of "natural," biological relations despite being composed of the contingent stuff of social and cultural forms. This sleight of hand, whereby the contingent is made to seem natural and essential, enables institutions to duplicate "the closed and tightly knit family structure that secures generational hierarchical relationships to one another" (21). In this way, Said explains how the radical possibility and open-endedness of affiliation reverts into reproducing the status quo by redrawing the lines of inclusion and exclusion. Filiation stubbornly remains in other forms: though modern society might diminish the significance of family bonds, they return in the form of a comforting nostalgia imbued in the non-biological, affiliative institutions that enable the reproduction of society.

In the previous section, I suggested that queer intergenerationality provokes the imagination of more sustainable futures by breaking with the filiative compulsion of heterosexual reproduction. This section complicates the argument by reading it through the lens of race: for many Indigenous and Black Studies scholars, the filiative metaphors of relationality and kinship play a significant role in knitting together humans and the environment through a shared sense of responsibility. Shawn Wilson (2008: 76), for example, writes that "We could not *be* without *being in relationship* with everything that surrounds us and is within us": he defines relationality as grounding Indigenous peoples "with the land, with their ancestors who have returned to the land and with future generations who will come into being on the land" (80).[26] Louise Erdrich's sterility dystopia, *Future Home of the Living God*, takes a critical approach to relationality by rejecting the role of reproductive filiation in the construction of an alternative social future. How does Indigenous relationality adapt to an attenuated future?

In the absence left behind by generational futurity, *Future Home* attends to the smaller timescale of the aging body, reimagining biological filiation as the self's transformation across time. Children and future generations occupy a privileged place in the Western imaginary because they support the biological fantasy of immortality by unspooling one's genetic material into eternity;[27] this fantasy, in turn, resonates with and naturalizes the capitalist desire of endless acquisition and extraction. Though similarly oriented toward the future, aging is alloyed with feelings of humiliation and fear: growing older implies temporal limits and the mortal necessity of an end. Yet it is precisely the temporal limitations of age that open the possibility for contingency, difference, and surprise. In what follows, I suggest that Erdrich's novel frames aging as a filiative process that functions in precisely the opposite way that Said outlines: instead of naturalizing or eternalizing affiliative social forms, growing older underlines their transience and contingency. This shift in perspective results in a more sobering definition of relationality that the one usually celebrated by critics. Greg Garrard (2023: 164–5) encourages critical scrutiny of accounts of Indigenous relationality as inherently and always ameliorative regardless of context: "Notions like 'respect' and 'relationship' can shift in meaning over time," he writes, and "scientific ecologists mostly reject [the] rhetoric" of

---

[26] Thomas King (1990: ix) writes that relationality constitutes a "web of kinship" that encourages "us to accept the responsibilities we have within the universal family by living our lives in a harmonious and moral manner (a common admonishment is to say of someone that they act as if they had no relations)."

[27] As I discuss in the previous section, what Sedgwick describes as: "it happened to my father's father, it happened to my father, it is happening to me, it will happen to my son, and it will happen to my son's son."

"'ecological balance' and Indigenous peoples' 'harmony' with nature." Erdrich's definition of relationality is similarly informed by the long shadow of prospective human extinction and environmental ruin: relationality arises as a response to what I call *senescent futurity*, a collective turn toward acknowledging vulnerability and care amid a diminishing future. Far from liquidating care of meaning (because its effects cannot be appreciated in the future), senescent futurity ennobles ephemerality as the basis for a modest and intentional social responsibility.

Race and Age in the Anthropocene

While climate change affects every human and non-human dwelling on the planet, scholars have shown that the universality of the calamity – while raising the stakes to terrifying and thus potentially actionable intensity – obscures the fact that its effects are felt at profoundly different magnitudes at the local level. Peter Wenz and Laura Westra (1995: xv) write in their introduction to *Faces of Environmental Racism* that "in the United States, poor people, African Americans, Hispanic Americans, and Native Americans suffer disproportionate exposure to environmental pollution." Stefania Barca (2020: 14) encourages us to view these environmental inequalities as a global problem: "extreme climate events are unevenly distributed across the planet and mostly concentrated in tropical and subtropical areas, which are among the world's poorest." Observing these racialized environmental disparities, Kathryn Yusoff (2018: xii) theorizes what she calls the "Black Anthropocene":

> The proximity of black and brown bodies to harm in . . . an inhuman proximity organized by historical geographies of extraction, grammars of geology, imperial global geographies, and contemporary environmental racism. It is predicated on the presumed absorbent qualities of black and brown bodies to take up the body burdens of exposure to toxicities and to buffer the violence of the earth.

For Yusoff, racism entails dehumanizing and sacrificing black and brown people for the sake of progress, modernity, and capitalism: racialized groups are both exposed to the brunt of environmental contamination and coerced into the practices that accelerate climate change. In the capitalist milieu, the racialized body absorbs environmental toxicity in a way that resembles how the aged body absorbs the depredations of time. The racialized body is also an aging body: attending to this intersection attunes us to the double marginalization of space and time, where the secreting of toxic waste around impoverished neighborhoods slowly accretes in the flesh of the racialized poor.

The pervasive effects of environmental racism have been obscured by the Anthropocene keyword: as the term soared in popularity, it quietly injected a universalizing liberal bias into environmental thought and activism.[28] The "term 'Anthropocene,'" Lauren Pulido (2018: 116) argues, "is a misnomer, as it obscures the fact that only a relatively small percentage of the global population is actually responsible for and has benefited from the conditions that produced it." Instead, she urges that "the Anthropocene must be seen as a racial process" (117). Seizing the land of Indigenous people for the sake of extracting resources, enslaving swathes of people to do the work of extraction: these racist practices not only underwrite the narrative of economic progress that apotheosizes to Western "civilization," but also remain largely invisible in critical accounts that emphasize the global aspect of the Anthropocene at the expense of its regional manifestations. To counter the universalizing tendency of the Anthropocene, Donna Harraway and Anna Tsing propose the term "Plantationocene" as a way of recentering the discussion on how colonization and slavery enabled the environmental devastation of global, large-scale terra-forming: "radical simplification; substitution of peoples, crops, microbes, and life forms; forced labor; and, crucially, the disordering of times of generation across species, including human beings" (Mitman, 2019). The displacement of slavery not only breaks the individual's connection to place, but also creates temporal shockwaves that interrupt "the possibility of the care of generations." Sterility dystopias, for example, often register environmental devastation by aligning the disruption of generations with the larger social and demographic transformations caused by anthropogenic change.

Scholars of racial ecology suggest that, in the wake of the Plantationocene and the disruption of generations, compensatory, affiliative structures arise in the form of relationality. Expanding upon Haraway's and Tsing's concept, the writers of "Anthropocene, Capitalocene, ... Plantationocene?" draw on Slyvia Wynter's analysis of the garden plot of slaves as an inspiration for forms of cooperation that challenge the racist logic of Plantation ecology: a zone where the runaway slaves intersected with black, white, and Indigenous abolitionists; a place to launch surreptitious expeditions to scavenge for food; an arena that encouraged multispecies wellbeing through "a spiritual code of reciprocity" (Davis et al., 2019: 8). The authors trace this legacy to the environmental justice

---

[28] As Marco Armiero (2021: 6) summarizes: "The main critique against the Anthropocene regards the alleged neutrality of the concept, its depoliticizing effect, its blindness toward social, historical, gender, and racial differences. The Anthropocene is the "age of humans," that is, an age in which "we" have affected the bio-geo-chemical cycles of the earth. Cohorts of progressive scholars have almost immediately signaled their discomfort with this universalistic narrative. For them – I should probably say for us – the "we" of the Anthropocene risks depicting humans as an undifferentiated community."

movement and urban centers of the present day, institutions that coalesce a community through, for example, education about the effects of toxic waste disposal near minorities. For these scholars, "relational modes of being" implies "multiple forms of kinship, and non-binary ways of engaging the world that foster ethics of care, equity, resilience, creativity, and sustainability" (8). Leanne Betasamosake Simpson (2021: 8) develops a similar line of argumentation from an Indigenous perspective, espousing "an ecology of relationships in the absence of coercion, hierarchy, or authoritarian power … connectivity based on the sanctity of the land, the love we have for our families, our language, our way of life. It is relationships based on deep reciprocity, respect, noninterference, self- determination, and freedom." Her concept of relationality resembles the rhizome rather than the hierarchical structures of Western civilization; furthermore, she rejects capital in favor of "accumulated networks of meaningful, deep, fluid, intimate collective and individual relationships of trust": "'Capital' in our reality isn't capital. We have no such thing as capital. We have relatives. We have clans. We have treaty partners. We do not have resources or capital" (77). When the currency that drives social meaning and cultural value shifts from the abstract and fungible medium of capital to the embodied relations of reciprocity and trust that link individuals together into collectives, "capital" is given a face. The death drive of extraction and endless acquisition cannot operate when capital wears the face of one's kin.

The face plays a central role in Habiba Ibrahim's (2021) work on the relation between age and race. She begins *Black Age* by reflecting on the disfigured face of Emmett Till, an African American boy who was lynched in Mississippi in 1955. Displayed from an open casket, Till's faceless corpse symptomized the separation of the black body "from its hegemonic relation to time": though a child, Till's fourteen-year-old body was reframed through racist discourse as a threatening, black adult male. As Ibrahim writes, "Black embodiment could be figured not only as childlike, but as any age at all. Black age is construable as anything because black subjects have been alienated from the time of their own bodies" (4). Through the racializing discourses of slavery and capitalism, blackness implies an age malleability that enables maximum exploitation – the child tried as an adult and sentenced to prison, the older person who can be simultaneously infantilized and forced to labor long past retirement age. As Ibrahim puts it, black age is "untimely": "existing in ways that run counter to dominant modalities of knowledge and reason" and laying claim to a "version of time that exceeds, transforms, or reinterprets western modern rationality" (29). Though black age entails placing the racialized subject outside insulating Western temporalities – in particular, the upward arc of liberal, developmental discourse – black age also creates the possibility to "to imagine the time of another humanity, beyond the time of Man" (6–7). From the malleability of black age, then, we arrive at the possibility of posthuman temporalities that challenge the dominant narrative that shapes how a human being ages over time.

Age has not played a significant role in the burgeoning scholarship on environmental racism. Urmi Willoughby (2021: 73), like the racial ecologists I cite above, acknowledges that studies "of global health show that threats to human health are most severe in poor regions and postcolonial states" and that "nonwhite populations are more at risk of suffering health consequences from environmental damage" (77). While scholars like Willoughby map race onto the uneven impacts of the environment on health, age allows us to better understand how this unevenness also takes temporal form – how the toxicity of environmental degradation slowly carves itself into the flesh of the body through premature aging, early puberty, chromosomal damage, and generational trauma. Age, race, and the environment intersect through the overdetermined issue of reproduction. Stefania Barca describes the class of "racialized, feminized, dispossessed" as "forces of reproduction: they keep the world alive, yet their environmental agency goes largely unrecognized in mainstream narratives of that epoch of catastrophic earth-system changes that scientists have called the Anthropocene" (1). Under late capitalism, the autotelic aspect of the labor that goes into reproducing life – from childbirth to the array of caregiving responsibilities needed to sustain it – has been commodified as "instruments for accumulation" (6). Reproducing life becomes an alienated or unwanted side-effect – a waste product – in the process of reproducing capital.

Black and Indigenous age plays a significant role in a racist strand of alarmist demography that contrasts the reproduction of youthful populations in the global South against the aging populations of the global North.[29] For Barca and Yusoff, Western society reproduces itself by forcing racialized populations to absorb the toxic excrescences of environmental exploitation. When the discourse shifts to demographic questions of age and *biological* reproduction, however, these same populations are situated as the cause, rather than the victim, of environmental harm. In the sterility dystopias where racialized aging intersects with ecological collapse, the temporality of human reproduction and crises of planetary scale intersect through the legacies of enslavement, diaspora, and eugenics. In Louise Erdrich's *Future Home*, for example, a new government based around racist, gendered, and religious chauvinism attempts to reproduce itself through the imprisonment of pregnant, Indigenous women.

---

[29] Frank Furedi (2002: xi) writes that "Concern with the decline of birth rates in the West is reinforced with fears about societies where fertility rates still remain high. Old preoccupations about competitive fertility have been recast as the threat faced by an ageing West from the younger and faster growing societies of the South."

Where my previous section argued for replacing the heteronormative passage of generations with the lateral ecology of queer intergenerationality, this section posits that racialized aging inspires equally transgressive approaches to the imagination of sustainable communities. Decoupling Edelman's association between futurity and the reproductive body, Jasbir Puar (2017: 211) draws our attention to the "biopolitics of regenerative capacity" that "demarcate racialized and sexualized statistical population aggregates as those in decay, destined for no future, based not upon whether they can or cannot reproduce children but on what capacities they can and cannot regenerate and what kinds of assemblages they compel, repel, spur, deflate." Alongside Puar's expansion of Edelman's argument to include racialized bodies, we must include the categories of older age and aging: for the biopolitical imagination, growing older shapes the reproductive futures for marginalized populations. If, as Habiba Ibrahim writes, the racialized body can be figured as any age, then racialized aging can also denaturalize the narrative of progress and succession that underwrites liberal modernity. At the intersection of race and age, we observe multiple futures that contest the singular, capitalist future of enrichment through the exploitation of fellow humans and extraction of the planet's resources.

Unlike *The Children of Men*, which frames saving the human race as a universal good, *Future Home* displays more ambivalence about the project of conserving humanity and the planet. The novel interrogates the specific definition of "the human" entailed in the liberal discourse of species preservation. To what end, and for whom, is the planet saved? For Erdrich, older age plays an important role in how she answers this question: to grow old is not a terrible outcome that requires either cultural repression or technological reparation. Rather, by viewing the final life stage neutrally, she critiques our dystopian tendency to project senescence onto macroscopic, complex entities like the species or the planet. Instead of symbolically concentrating the doomed energies of the Anthropocene, older age provides the starting point for alternative solutions to climate change that extend beyond the Western deferral for a technological panacea in an ever-receding future or a Romanticized return to a pre-modern past that nostalgically recalls the unsullied days of childhood and clean, blue skies. In contrast, Erdrich imagines our senescent future through the perspective of the racialized subjects most impacted by the crisis. Doing so posits radically different solutions: instead of funding research for a technological breakthrough to stop aging or climate change, to direct *care* to the most vulnerable parts of society and the environment; instead of turning inward to the solutions of the past that have precipitated the crisis, to look outward to the radically alien and Other for alternatives; instead of privileging the liberal individual, to embrace Indigenous forms of relationality and collectivity that embed vulnerability and dependence into the society rather than excluding them as humiliating aberrations; instead of using demographics as a way of rationalizing inequities, to break with the hierarchical and possessive behaviors that link individuals into a grasping relation with both time (to claw back years) and place (to extract every resource).

Through the lens of age and race, therefore, the temporal and spatial modalities of the environment intersect in profoundly different ways than they do from the perspective of the Western liberal individual. What does it mean to inhabit a senescent futurity? A future that contests the relentless, teleological drive toward productivity and accumulation by privileging the slow, autotelic states of reflection, contentment, and care? While the senescent futurity of a dystopic civilization in decline has little value according to capitalist modernity, it affords opportunities of social and environmental reparation for racialized and marginalized subjects.

No Future Home

> First the cold didn't burn your lungs, said Sera. The cold didn't freeze the snot in your nose, didn't frost your eyelashes, didn't hurt, said Glen. And the snow didn't squeak underneath your footsteps or against the car's tires. Soon the cold stopped pinching, stopped running its fingers up your back, stopped numbing your face, your fingers. The snow still came down in fluffy flakes sometimes. Once or twice it was finely suspended in the wind and we tried to call it a blizzard. But it was only here a moment. Next winter, it rained. The cold was mild and refreshing. But only rain. That was the year we lost winter. Lost our cold heaven.
>
> -Louise Erdrich, *Future Home of the Living God* (336)

Near the end of Louise Erdrich's *Future Home*, the novel's protagonist Cedar Hawk Songmaker reflects on the changing climate from her incarceration in a facility where women are forcefully inseminated to replenish the population. She remembers the creep of rising temperatures as a gradual loosening of winter's painful grip. It stops pinching and numbing. The "mild and refreshing" rain that replaces winter does not provide comfort; instead, it registers the trace of the "cold heaven" that has been lost. The burning, pinching, and numbing comprise the rough language of winter's communion with the human body. The rising temperatures sever the conduit of painful sympathy that links the individual to her "cold heaven," replacing it with the temperate rains of climate change that belie their tremendous danger. The warming climate forms one aspect of the larger evolutionary backsliding that underwrites the novel's plot: for as temperatures rise, turning the earth into a primordial greenhouse, the flora and fauna of earth revert to atavistic forms or take on less complexity. The Minnesotan plant life tropicalizes, the domestic cat bulks into something resembling the predatory sabretooth. While human women still become pregnant, birth often results in maternal death, birth defects, and stillbirth. As in Margaret Atwood's *The Handmaid's Tale*, the demographic anxiety arising from the scarcity of human babies precipitates the backsliding of American society into evangelical authoritarianism. Under the guise of paternalist care, the new government – the Church of the New Constitution – forces "pregnant women [to] be sequestered into hospitals in order to give birth under controlled circumstances" (92).

The problem with reproduction in *Future Home* is not fully explained: "nobody knows," the narrator writes, except "our world is running backward. Or forward. Or maybe sideways, in a way as yet ungrasped" (3). The linear narrative of liberal progress that structures most aspects of Western society – from the economic fantasy of endless accumulation and the biological dream of immortality through future generations – comes to an abrupt halt. Time continues, but not in a straight line. Most characters in the novel process the end of linear development as backwardness. Indeed, linearity is deeply embedded as a structuring binary in the ideology of modernity: if the individual or society is not moving forward, then they are moving backward. She watches a television program sentimentalize the evolutionary crisis through hackneyed Darwinian tropes and the degeneration of Western culture's greatest achievements: "And meanwhile the station has invented a swirling set of graphics – humanoid figures growing hunched as they walked into the mists of time, while in the background Beethoven's Fifth Symphony dissolves into a haunting series of hoots and squawks" (66). However, Cedar remains open to the possibility of competing temporal modalities – that different models of progress exist outside of linear development, that moving "backward" in time implies forms of forward movement that the dominant culture rejects, that "sideways" or lateral temporalities also constitute valid models of time. According to Sally Grande (2018: 174), Indigenous aging is structured according to "cycles of life(s), not temporally ordered along a linear lifespan": for Alaska Natives, the title of elder is not "based on chronological age, but rather is a designation or honor bestowed by the community." Wendy Hulko's (2010: 330) interviews of the Secwepemc First Nations peoples attests to an orbital model where one ages backward to an original spirit world: "Elders and infants are both close to the spirit world; the infants arriving from it, and the elders traveling to it."

Like these accounts of Indigenous aging, Cedar's father, Glen, observes that the very idea of evolution going backward and reforming the human species into its "hunched" ancestors relies upon a temporal fallacy that anything other than linear development will retrace the same steps in the opposite direction:

> So if evolution has actually stopped, which is by no means fact, it is only
> speculation, and if evolution is going backward, which is still only an
> improbable idea, then we would not see the orderly backward progression
> of human types that evolutionary charts are so fond of presenting. Life might
> skip forward, sideways, in unforeseen directions. We wouldn't see the narra-
> tive we think we know. Why? Because there was never a story moving
> forward and there wouldn't be one moving backward. (69)

Glen demystifies the narrative that links evolution to increasing complexity. Even
in the novel's accelerated evolution toward simplicity, time continues to move
forward – the transformations that occur to species will not form a mirror image
of evolutionary development but strike out in surprising new directions. Andreas
Hejnol (2017: G91) asserts that the ladders and trees that organize biological life
in terms of "hierarchical relationships among living species" produce a misguided
sense of how evolution functions. Drawing on the example of tunicates evolving
to a state of lesser complexity, he suggests that cladistics and the comparison of
molecular data among species "strengthens the deconstruction of the teleological
elements in the understanding of the processes in evolution, including hierarchical orderings of beings … they also demonstrate that evolution itself is nondi-
rectional and unpredictable" (G91). In the words of Glen, "there was never a story
moving forward and there wouldn't be one moving backward." Nevertheless,
American society remains committed to grafting the cultural narrative of linear
progress onto the timescale of evolution. In *Future Home*, the regression of the
American government to an authoritarian regime writes large the importance of
this evolutionary narrative of societal progress in validating the violence that
marginalizes Others – without these hierarchical exclusions, liberal society would
not have access to the cheap labor needed to reproduce itself.[30]

The hierarchical exclusions that reproduce liberal society are drawn along the
axes of race, class, and gender – as that society becomes threatened, it draws the
lines that distinguish "us" from "them" in increasingly stark and violent ways.
Subtle changes in television programming herald the tyrannical government of
The Church of the New Constitution:

> The women are fewer, the ones who appear seem awkward, all in their twenties,
> white with white teeth, yellow or brown hair, sparkling eyes. The men are all
> white with white teeth, sharp jawlines, sparkling eyes.… There are no brown
> people, anywhere, not in movies not on sitcoms not on shopping channels or on
> the dozens of evangelical channels up and down the remote. (56)[31]

---

[30] Moreover, the narrative insulates the dominant regime from the threat of counterfactual possibilities – self-fashioned as the telos of history and social evolution, white, liberal society is the
only and best possible outcome. Things could not have been different from the way they are.

[31] The tyrannical Church of the New Constitution takes the embodied form of "Mother," an avatar
of the white, evangelical, middle class that surveils through electronic devices.

Through the cultural engineering of casting, the dominant regime naturalizes the infantilization of women and the absence of people of color. The disappearance of women and black and brown people from all forms of media serves as the first step to their disappearance from the public sphere of liberal society. The rights of women to freedom and self-determination are swept away through the policy of "gravid female detention" that enables the incarceration of all pregnant women (93). A militant group raids an in-vitro clinic to gestate the stolen embryos using one thousand "Womb Volunteers": on the radio, the leader reports that "'We took the leftovers. The embryos not labeled Caucasian. We're going to have them all and keep them all. We're not killing any. All are sacred" (114). The doublespeak thinly conceals the coercion behind "volunteers" and the racist contempt behind the word "sacred." To the speaker, the non-Caucasian "leftovers" are sacred only in the sense of a sacrifice, which is enabled *because* of the embryos' racialization not *in spite* of it.

Race and ethnicity play an important role in the way *Future Home* represents competing modes of relationality. For The Church of the New Constitution, that relation is carceral: ensconced in her hospital-prison, Cedar observes the motivational slogans of the State: "Accept life. You can be absolved or anything you did, you can completely win back God's love, by contributing to the future of humanity. Your happy sentence is only nine months" (321). The prison de-filiates Cedar, separating her from the kinship network that gives her life meaning and pleasure. Instead, the state coerces her into a relation with the "future of humanity" – a faceless abstraction that she will never know or love.[32] The nurses seize Cedar's child immediately after birth, further severing any sympathetic investment in the "future of humanity." The deracinating and universalizing "future of humanity" underwrites the specific brand of white, patriarchal society that seeks to reproduce itself through the instrumentalization of racialized women's bodies. The very expansiveness and ambiguity of this white futurity, which trails off into the mists of eternity, provides one of the ideological pillars for the capitalist temporality of endless acquisition and growth. The racialized labor of biological reproduction furnishes the capitalist unconscious with dreams of fecundity and excess while, at the same time, requiring strict reproductive control to maintain existing hierarchies.

The father of Cedar's child, Phil, exemplifies another mode of white temporal relationality: crisis. Though he initially attempts to protect Cedar from the government, Phil is captured, tortured, and eventually reveals her hiding place. When Cedar and Phil reunite later in the novel, he has changed: "After all, it's a global

---

[32] The wall of the prison lists the birth and death of each inmate, framing her as a martyr for the same cold, abstraction of time as the "future of humanity": "And below that a line that says: *She served the future*" (320).

crisis, it's the future of humanity, so you can see why they need to keep an eye on women" (310). Parroting the "future of humanity" slogan, Phil draws on the urgency of the global crisis as a way of justifying the incarceration of women and people of color. Kyle Powys Whyte (2020) suggests that crisis rhetoric draws on a colonial discourse that validates oppression by framing the experience of the present as new, unprecedented, and urgent. Whyte reads the legacy of colonial power through examples of climate change activism and policy. "Presumptions of urgency," he writes, "generat[e] harm and risks that burden Indigenous peoples, and retrench colonial power" (56): "climate change, as a concept, is a rhetorical device that people invoke so they can believe they are addressing a crisis without having to talk about colonial power" (57). In Erdrich's novel, Phil is a committed environmentalist with a philosophy: "Do no harm, to anything or anyone. Save nature. He decided to dedicate himself to preserving bird habitat, and got an advanced degree in ecology. Since then, he has tried to protect the natural world wherever possible. Without being specific, he told me that he's gone beyond the law" (106). Crisis epistemology informs both Phil's environmentalism and his response to evolutionary backwardness: though he agrees with the liberal injunction to "do no harm" and engages in the laudable effort of preservation, the crisis creates states of exception that direct harm to the most vulnerable members of society. The presentist myopia of the crisis "absents the violence and tribulations of diverse ancestors" and, in the process of "saving" them, visits harm on "living and future generations" (Whyte 2020: 55).

In contrast to crisis, Whyte (2020: 58) offers epistemologies of coordination that "emphasize coming to know the world through kin relationships" such as "care, consent, and reciprocity." Whyte (2021: 45) offers the idea of "kinship time" as an alternative to the ticking clock of "linear, sequential time" used to imbue the climate crisis with a sense of peril. He proposes that "we start telling time through the duration, span, and movement of kinship relationships. When time is experienced through kinship, the ticking clock goes away. Duration is perceived according to the degree of current kinship relationships, the history of kinship relationships, and future possibilities of kinship relationships" (2021: 49). Cedar's narrative follows the arc of kinship time: adopted by white, middle-class parents, Cedar begins the novel by reaching out to her biological mother, an Ojibwe woman living on a reservation. As she learns more about her biological mother, Mary Potts (better known as Sweetie), Cedar's kinship network grows.[33] After an awkward meeting between her two families, Cedar learns that her

---

[33] Through the name of Mary Potts, Cedar speculates about her genealogy back to the beginning of colonization: "I was Mary Potts, daughter and granddaughter of Mary Potts, big sister to another Mary Potts, in short, just another of many Mary Potts reaching back to the colonization of this region, many of whom now worked at the Superpumper franchise first stop before the casino" (6).

adoptive father has been her biological father all along: the new relations intensify and transform old ones. Though kinship time can open one to painful revelations, such as the disclosure of Cedar's biological father, it also offers something significant in return: knowledge of the past, a new relation, possibilities for the future, all of which can be fit (albeit in sometimes awkward ways) into the matrix of a constantly evolving relationality. Kinship time introduces new and different relations into one's sphere of care and reciprocity: opposed to the lockstep of generations, kinship time remains open to change as the quantity, intensity, and duration of one's relationships change.

Crisis rhetoric – such as the "future of humanity" or the "global crisis" – makes exclusion a structural principle: the future of humanity envisions a future for a privileged class of human, while the global crisis will disproportionately affect another, marginal one. However, the crisis loses its power if the demarcation between privileged and marginal breaks down, which is precisely what the evolving relations of kinship threaten to do. The boyfriend of Cedar's biological mother, Eddy, spends the first half of the novel working at a gas station and writing a memoir that catalogues the different reasons he has not committed suicide. A Harvard PhD in education with ambitions to reform the school system on the reservation, Eddy lapses into depression after his efforts at improvement are unsuccessful. Referencing the evolutionary event, he tells Cedar that "All my life I've sensed an unseen deterioration.... I've always known that this was happening. It has colored my mental processes and been the reason for all that I have written. I have waited for it and known that it, or something like it, would come" (34). Eddy exists in an anticipatory relation to the present, perceiving the "unseen deterioration" that festers under the façade of normalcy, and yet he is unable to convince others that his narrative reflects reality.[34] His knowledge of how present practices will affect the future creates a social asynchrony: branded as an eccentric and failure, he spends most of his time alone behind the register of the gas station. When his premonition of deterioration is validated by the evolutionary event, he takes on the leadership role of organizing the Ojibwe in a self-sustaining collective: "he looks tougher. He looks straight on at people now.... His stare, when it focuses on a person, is long-seeing" (287). The transformation of American society into the Church of the New Constitution confirms his dark presentiment, and as his knowledge accords with the state of the world he becomes more confident in his sense of self: "I think about seventy percent of my depression was my seventeenth-century warrior trying to get out" (287). When Eddy perceives the canker at the

---

[34] Eddy serves as a good example of the asynchrony that Kyle Powys Whyte (2017: 207) diagnoses in "Our Ancestors' Dystopia Now": "some indigenous peoples already inhabit what our ancestors would have likely characterized as a dystopian future."

heart of American society, he is gaslighted as untimely – an eccentric, severed from the kinship of his own people. When Eddy gains confidence in his understanding of time, however, a matrix of Indigenous relationality emerges: he encourages ex-gangsters to grow cannabis seedlings in the aisles of the casino, young people to learn how to farm pigs, cows, and chickens, veterans to train warriors to protect the community.

The loss of Minnestota's "cold heaven" and evolutionary backwardness take the social form of a regression to patriarchal authoritarianism and tyranny: the degradation of the environment and of American society progress slowly and quietly enough to avoid general outcry. Only sensitive people like Eddy register the "unseen deterioration," and his intuition is repressed through social ostracism. Both environmental and social decline fester beneath the collective threshold of perception: once the effects of climate change and tyranny manifest themselves, it is too late to implement the practices to reverse the processes. It is much better to prevent the rise of global temperatures by 1.5 degrees Celsius than attempt to reduce it by the same amount; similarly, it is much better to build strong institutions to prevent an authoritarian government than unseat one already in power. The novel attests to the problem of belatedness: once the effects are felt, it is already too late to address the causes. Too late: the ticking clock of crisis did not even have a chance to wind up.

In Erdrich's dystopian future, belatedness takes the large-scale forms of environmental and social dysfunction. These large-scale manifestations of belatedness, however, draw upon the intimate experience of growing older for their legibility and affective force. In *Aging, Duration, and the English Novel* (2020: 1–2), I identify a literary tendency to collapse the duration of aging into epiphanic moments: "the rapid onset of dementia after an illness, the development of gray hair after a traumatic loss, the sudden appearance of a wrinkle in the brow of a spurned lover," these recognitions often take place all at once while a character observes themselves in front of a mirror. Representations of growing older follow a larger cultural tendency to repress the process of aging: the shocking recognition of one's aging registers the belatedness of time's passage, and we are trained to recognize aging in the past tense and ignore its duration in the present. This unhealthy relation to our embodied temporality scales up to the way we understand environmental and social temporalities, which we similarly repress until it is "too late" to address the causes that culminate in ecological devastation and social inequities. From the most personal experience of temporality, our aging, we extrapolate a model of time that underwrites the macrocosmic assemblages of environmental and social policy. Thus, how the individual and culture frame aging, whether they take a critical or uncritical approach, has significant repercussions for the way time maps onto the social body and the planet as a whole. This argument hinges on a dubious organicism that maps, by means of analogy, biological processes onto inorganic and social ones. Yet Erdrich's *Future Home* anticipates exactly this move through the linked backwardness of evolution and social institutions: the reduction of biological complexity occurs alongside the return of superannuated forms of governance. This is Erdrich's view of the belatedness of our modernity: the vestiges of old misogyny and racism have not been overcome by liberal society but form integral parts of its structure. The aging society of the sterility dystopia writes large the collective shock that arises when such violent prejudices inevitably bubble to the surface. Like the individual who stares in amazement at the appearance of a wrinkle or gray hair, we are forced to confront, always too late, the spectacular effects of ignoring slow accretions of social and environmental inequity.

Erdrich theorizes the relational temporality of Indigenous aging to counter the belatedness of liberal capitalism, which represses the process of aging until its effects become shockingly evident. In contrast to the modernization of older age, which entails framing the "elderly" as an economic burden to society, Indigenous societies tend to provide a stronger support network for older people: roles that accord older people with value and dignity, cultural narratives that reinforce the importance of experience and perspective. Sally Grande observes that within "Indigenous communities elders have always held places of distinction as knowledge keepers, spiritual and political leaders, and attendants of past, present, and future generations" (169).[35] The joint family of the Mary Potts's household, which includes three generations ranging from a teenager to a 128-year-old grandmother, provides an example of this. Indigenous aging, however, goes beyond the social to encourage a deeper relationality with oneself. Instead of the continuous, Lockean self glued together through memory over time, Indigenous aging implies a heterogeneous assemblage of selves resembling a kinship network. The differences that emerge between one's younger and older self are not existential discrepancies but the discrete facets of a larger, vibrant, embodied collectivity. Late in the novel, Sweetie presents a picture of her younger self after giving birth to Cedar, just before offering her daughter for adoption: an image of a punk festooned with piercings, "bright yellow-green hair," and smeared makeup, incongruously surrounded by flowers and Mylar

---

[35] In interviews older members of the Secwepemc Nation, Wendy Hulko (et al.) report that "Elders spoke of moving into importance as they grew older" (326). Donna Granbois and Gregory Sanders (2009: 576) transcribe the following from an interview with an Elder named Taowhywee: The Elders "are the wisdom keepers, for God's sake, and they have a lot of things to say. It is through them that you get strength, through that grandma and that grandma and that grandfather and that grandfather. They are all inside of you, each and every one, every human on this earth."

balloons (278). Rather than disavow this younger self as an aberration, Sweetie acknowledges her as kin: a relation on the "crooked and wild" path of her life (279). She does not feel the shock of non-recognition – how could I have changed this much? – and belatedly attempt to retrofit her younger and older selves through the narrative of conversion. Rather, they sidle alongside each other across the span of years, discrete personalities tethered to the same body.

The endurance of Cedar's long-lived grandmother, Virginia, provides a resonant counterpoint to the reproductive crisis that afflicts society: "'Hundred and twenty-eight,' says a reedy little voice from around the corner. A tiny, brown, hunched-up little lady then wheels herself incrementally – she's wheeling herself on carpet – around the corner" (22). Grandma Virginia's longevity is matched by her late pregnancy, as her daughter Sweetie recounts that "She had me when she was fifty-three, no lie, remember that. Use condoms until you're sixty, ha!" (22). Though Grandma Virginia occupies a minor role throughout most of the novel, she tells a story that Cedar includes in her epistolary narrative: this short story, "The Fat Man's Race," appears just after Cedar learns the identity of her biological father, and begins with Grandma's observation that "Men are tricky" (296). She relates the story of her love of Cuthbert, a large man whose fortune matches his prodigious appetite. But as they plan the wedding, a man in a blue suit, blue shirt, blue tie, and blue shoes – her devil, she says – makes love to Virginia in her dreams every night. Her desire for the man in blue is matched by her repulsion when she wakes, and she eventually dreams a knife to kill the devil while she sleeps. On the feast day of the Assumption, the large men line up to compete in the titular race – the devil appears next to Cuthbert and the two race to the finish line, only to perish side by side. Grandma Virginia explains the moral:

> I married instead a man who hadn't an ounce of spare flesh, a man who hated the color blue and never wore it.... I lived with him for fifty-seven years now, didn't I, and the two of us had eight children. Adopted twenty. Raised every kind of animal that you can think of, didn't we, and grew our corn and oats and every fall dug our hills of potatoes. We picked wild rice. (300)

The story makes for a bizarre interlude – in contrast to the form of the novel's epistolary memoir, it is a fable enriched with the fantastic and dreamlike. It is autobiographical, though not written in the style or tone of Grandma Virginia's voice. While the content is about "tricky" men, it focuses on lovers instead of fathers. In contrast to the sterile world represented in Cedar's narrative, the story's conclusion with fecundity and abundance feels dissonant and off key. If we focus on Grandma Virginia's age, it might appear as nothing more than a senile interruption or digression. As a kind of refracting mirror, the story enables Cedar to confront her own life narrative: "Grandma's story completely diverts me from the sudden reversals in my own narrative. It also feels like a warning. My father and mother, both loving and lying to me. And Phil, my angel of deception" (301). Such reversals include the revelation that her adoptive father, Glen, is both "more" of a father through blood and yet less through deceit; that her husband, Phil, is both the father of her child and an instrument for the state's reproductive control. The story interrupts the paralysis that arises from these inconsistencies, consoling Cedar with the possibility of the vibrant, fecund future that concludes Grandma Virginia's story.

Joni Adamson and Salma Monani (2017: 3) would likely characterize Grandma Virginia's story as an "indigenous 'cosmovision'": a conception "of entangled human relations with more-than-human worlds." They write that "Such 'native slipstream' or 'space-time thinking' is particularly valuable as a means to confront Western notions of linear progress, which not only tend to ignore the cyclic rhythms of earth's bio-geomorphic systems but do so with dangerously myopic focus" (15). Indeed, the reversals in Cedar's life narrative form personal manifestations of the larger evolutionary reversal that underwrites the plot of the novel. The men who compete for Grandma Virginia are two sides of excessive consumption – in the daylight, Cuthbert grows fat from eating hunks of venison and whole chickens, while at night, the man in the blue suit charms his way into the bed of multiple women. As facets of the same drive, the two men destroy each other through the competition of the race, underlining the ridiculously self-destructive logic behind the desire to possess and consume. The death of the two men warns against the same patterns of unchecked desire. Grandma Virginia, in contrast, (re)produces: she gives birth to eight children and adopts twenty, she raises all types of animals and crops. And she picks wild rice, a sacred food staple for Indigenous groups in the Minnesota region that has declined by half in the last one hundred years through "mining, damming, growing commercial paddy rice for mass distribution, and recreational boating" (Whyte, 2017: 211).

Grandma Virginia's great age of 128 provides a portal to a time when wild rice proliferated: a planet scarred by industrialization yet not radically transformed by the great acceleration. Through the cosmovision her past becomes a possible future: evolutionary reversal might terrify the proponents of progress, but it also serves as a means of Indigenous reparation as the new bustle of life on the reservation attests. In this new world, the "fat man's race" is a deadly competition for the young who wear themselves out prematurely through their endless desire for more. Grandma Virginia endures, however, and her story celebrates the irruption of kinship across filiative and affiliative relations, across human and non-human entities. She envisions a senescent futurity where time itself is relational – not as a linear narrative of overcoming, but as the assemblage of past, present, and future as kin, joined through the same kind of affective links and reciprocities that hold families and collectives together: the titular *future home*. The Indigenous future of Erdrich's novel is senescent not because it is old and decrepit, but because it suggests that the future requires care and a sense of responsibility – it emphasizes that, given enough time, we will age into that future: we have (s)kin in the game. Moreover, senescent futurity recognizes that decline and reversal might provide the best temporalities for navigating the environmental crises of modernity: a return to pastures of wild rice rather than industrial agriculture. Confronting the overwhelmingly negative connotations associated with senescence, decline, backwardness, and reversal is part of the challenge; the terms require us to engage with vulnerability as a condition of existence, a matter of time, rather than a reason for exploitation.

Intimations of Extinction

The sterility dystopias that I analyze in this Element register the genre's complex approach to aging and the environment. Some emphasize global despair while others identify openings for large-scale transformation. Often, children reappear and the whole machine starts humming again, much to everyone's satisfaction. Yet in forcing the reader to reckon with a world without children, the genre also challenges the reader to reflect on their anthropocentric assumptions about the world. How do we understand or feel about Earth when it is no longer understood as a dwelling place for humans? The sterility dystopia, in its explicit and implicit relation between human reproduction and the environment, suggests that universal infertility is both a consequence and a symptom of the fact that extractive capitalism has never treated the earth as a dwelling place for humans in the first place. The individuals and corporations most implicated in the capitalist practices of planetary destruction are, by necessity, the most unreflectively confident in Earth's habitability for future human generations. The work of ideology critique, drawing out the inconsistencies in capitalist practice and belief, has not converted many from this camp. Reading sterility dystopia fiction will probably not convince them either.

This Element, instead, articulates senescent environmentalism to reframe some of the temporal assumptions of ecocritical thought and practice. Like the celebration of the child's innocent and unmediated experience of nature, a popular strand of environmentalist literature draws on the figure of purity to conjure nostalgia for the undamaged ecosystems of the past. In contrast, senescent environmentalism acknowledges that planetary reparations will grapple with centuries of engrained damage. The best technology and social policy will not erase the traces left behind by anthropogenic change. Anna Tsing (2015: 3) focuses on the possibilities that arise from the legacy of capitalist extraction, finding inspiration in the matsutake mushrooms that thrive in the "blasted landscapes" of human-disturbed forests: "In a global state of precarity," she writes, "we don't have choices other than looking for life in this ruin" (6). Older age offers a temporal, rather than spatial, way of surviving amid the ruins. It reminds us that, while we cannot return to the past, our accumulated experience can build a more equitable and sustainable future – if our culture and society values that experience. Older age attunes us to transience and contingency, the delicacy of ecosystems on the brink, the structural precarity of marginalized individuals in societies across the globe. It symbolically concentrates our collective vulnerability as we anxiously wait before the end we know is coming.

I conclude with a discussion of William Wordsworth's ([1807] 2002) "Ode: Intimations of Immortality" because, by seeming to oppose everything I have argued in this volume, the poem draws out both the challenges and the necessity for a senescent environmentalism. Where the sterility dystopia imagines a future without children, Wordsworth's poem nostalgically remembers a past charged with the utopian immediacy of his childhood:

> There was a time when meadow, grove, and stream,
>   The earth, and every common sight,
>   To me did seem
>   Apparelled in celestial light,
>   The glory and the freshness of a dream.
> It is not now as it hath been of yore; –
>   Turn wheresoe'er I may,
>   By night or day,
> The things which I have seen I now can see no more. (1–9)

As the poet grows older, the "glory and the freshness" departs from his perception of the natural world: though his eye alights upon the same "meadow, grove, and stream," the poet cannot experience – again – the affective core of such "common sight[s]" because of the time that divides his younger and mature self. A significant loss occurs during the interval of aging. The poet speculates that, as the infant's soul is closest in temporal proximity to the divine, it is most imbued with the "trailing clouds of glory" (64): "Heaven lies about us in our infancy!" the poet exclaims (66). As the infant grows into a boy and a youth, "the prison-house begin to close" until "At length the Man perceives it die away" (67, 75). The poem crystallizes an ageist assumption that underwrites a powerful, Romantic narrative that persists from the nineteenth century to the present day: while the child can experience the world as invested with something like the divine, growing older involves becoming dull and worldly. In the Wordsworthian idiom, the abundant terrestrial pleasures of the earth serve as distractions from the wonder and sublimity of nature. In the twenty-first century, we might gesture to the bewildering spectacles of consumer capitalism that leave behind nothing but the contentless trace of their evanescent existence.

Yet the child continually gropes toward the attenuated experience of adult life through play and mimicry, acting out the cultural milestones of a human life: a "wedding" (94), "festival" "funeral" (95), "business" (99), and "love" (99). The youth, moreover, plays at every stage of the human lifespan:

> The little Actor cons another part;
> Filling from time to time his "humorous stage"
> With all the Persons, down to palsied Age,
> That Life brings with her in her equipage;
> As if his whole vocation
> Were endless imitation. (103–8)

Alluding to Jacques's monologue in William Shakespeare's (2008: 151) *As You Like It* – "All the world's a stage, / And all the men and women merely players" – Wordsworth's "little Actor" *performs the performance of a life stage on life's stage*. This should be understood not so much as training for these future roles, but as a way of drawing out the temporal ironies of childhood: that the adult stages of life where wonder has departed can be proleptically experienced as wonderful through the child's performance; that the duration that holds together and linearizes human life stages can be compressed and disorganized through play; that the desire of a child at the beginning of life would be to enact the "palsied Age" at the end. It is the last stage of life that Wordsworth highlights, the one upon which Jacques heaps the most scorn: "Last scene of all, / That ends this strange eventful history, / Is second childishness and mere oblivion, / Sans teeth, sans eyes, sans taste, sans everything" (151–2). In contrast to Jacques's description of the faults and follies of other life stages – the infant's mewling, the schoolboy's whining, the soldier's haste – older age is defined by nullity and lack. Older age is not just defined negatively, it is defined *as* negativity: an apocalypse of identity. Read in relation to Jacques's monologue, the Wordsworthian child's imitation of older age is more than a way of anticipating the bodily transformations that occur as one ages. The performance of the child imbues the categorical nullity of senescence with the same wonder that defines his experience of the natural world, so that even the most dreaded time of the human lifespan gains something from the child's affective depth and richness of experience.

As Wordsworth imagines that children arrive in the world "trailing clouds of glory" from their heavenly provenance, popular representations of older people tend to situate them as trailing clouds of dust, decay, and ruin. Where Wordsworth's child performs the role of "palsied Age," older people are widely believed to imitate the child through what Jacques describes as "second childishness." Where, for Wordsworth, the youthful performance of older age infuses the latter stage with affective depth, the senescent performance of childhood inverts the logic: from this perspective, the stereoscopic richness of childish play flattens out into pointless, repetitive exercises. Where the child engages in autotelic play, the older person shrinks from the anticipated end: the value and urgency of forestalling death exponentially increasing in relation to the perceived proximity of that end. In the depopulating and aging world of the sterility dystopia, Wordsworth's child has been usurped by the senescent horseman of the apocalypse, who, like the speaker of the "Ode," reflects nostalgically on a past world that looks uncannily familiar but no longer exists. The genre replaces intimations of immortality with extinction: for if the Wordsworthian child perceives the divine in nature, the older dystopian not only perceives the loss of this faculty in herself, but also grapples with the bitter realization that such perception has been lost to the world forever. Without children, the world is all there is.

In demystifying the Romanticized relation between the child and the natural world, the sterility dystopia engineers a difficult confrontation with the brute materiality of a planet under duress. I have argued throughout this volume that the sterility dystopia desacralizes the child as the carrier of future possibility and offers a temporally neutral perspective of the human lifespan (as I discuss through Derek Parfit's work in the section "Queer Genre/ations" above). A great deal of environmentalist discourse frames the urgency of climate action as the means of preserving future generations. It is for the sake of the future – children alive and yet unborn – that we are urged to take collective action. In pushing against this narrative and decoupling the figurative connection between futurity and children, I open the possibility of non-linear and non-teleological futures that include the non-reproductive bodies of older people and queers. Rather than the obsessive drive to secure the future, I propose the non-hierarchical immediacy of queer intergenerationality: the collectives, activist groups, and shared dialogues that arise from a network of individuals linked through care for one another and the world they inhabit. When we decenter the heteronormative orientation toward reproductive futurity as the *only, best,* or *default* option, we also displace the capitalist rationalization of environmental exploitation for the sake of an imagined future of enormous profits and infinite accumulation. In contrast to capital's anticipatory hyperopia, the attenuated future of queer intergenerationality inspires a granular attention to the present that, ironically, nurtures a sustainable future into existence.

Senescent environmentalism also intersects with the work of racial ecologists, enabling alternative ways of conceptualizing racialized temporalities in the Anthropocene. Rather than competition, crisis, and progress, Indigenous forms of relational temporality urge collaboration, patience, and kinship. Where liberal progress always entails leaving someone behind – usually marginalized groups of women and people of color – a relational temporality moves into the future slowly because it carries the entire kinship group with it. Indeed, a relational temporality blurs the distinctions between past, present, and future as the tenses are all temporal kin, after all. The senescent futurity of Erdrich's *Future Home*, embodied in Cedar's 128-year-old tale-telling grandmother, activates the necessity for care and responsibility; it does so, not only through the figure of Grandma Virginia, but by provoking the reader into a confrontation with his or her own temporary independence. If we are lucky, we look forward to the inevitability of our senescent future, one that demands sympathy – or kinship – with that older self we will one day become. The very temporalities that oppose modern "progress" are often used to stigmatize the racialized groups and older people who impede Western "civilization": decline, backwardness, stasis. These temporalities of the marginal and dispossessed contest a model of human flourishing based on limitless growth and enable the imagination of a more sustainable, senescent future.

References

Adamson, Joni and Salma Monani. (2017). Introduction: Cosmovisions, Ecocriticism, and Indigenous-Studies. In J. Adamson and S. Monani, eds., *Ecocriticism and Indigenous Studies: Conversations from Earth to Cosmos*, London: Routledge, pp. 1–19.

Ahuja, Neel. (2015). Intimate Atmospheres: Queer Theory in a Time of Extinctions. *GLQ*, 21(2–3), 365–85.

Aldiss, Brian. (2011). *Greybeard (The Children of Men)*, London: Orion.

Armiero, Marco. (2021). *Wasteocene: Stories from the Global Dump*, Cambridge: Cambridge University Press.

Atwood, Margaret. (1996). *The Handmaid's Tale*, London: Vintage.

Barca, Stefania. (2020). *Forces of Reproduction: Notes for a Counter-Hegemonic Anthropocene*, Cambridge: Cambridge University Press.

Birchley, Emma. (2019). Extinction Rebellion: 91-Year-Old Climate Protester Arrested Near Port of Dover. *Sky News*, September 21. https://news.sky.com/story/extinction-rebellion-91-year-old-climate-protester-arrested-near-port-of-dover-11815748#:~:text=Demonstrators%20had%20aimed%20to%20blockade,because%20of%20the%20climate%20crisis.&text=A%2091%2Dyear%2Dold%20man%20is%20among%2010%20people%20who,with%20climate%20activists%20Extinction%20Rebellion

Bloch, Ernst. (1986). *The Principle of Hope*, Vol. I, Cambridge, MA: MIT Press.

Buell, Lawrence. (2016). Anthropocene Panic: Contemporary Ecocriticism and the Issue of Human Numbers. *Frame*, 29(2), 11–27.

Butler, Octavia E. (2007). *Lilith's Brood*, New York: Grand Central.

Byrne, Clodagh Clare Harris, Mark Gorman et al. (2015). Climate Change in an Ageing World. *Help Age Position Paper*, London: Help Age International, pp. 1–12.

Chakrabarty, Dipesh. (2019). The Planet: An Emergent Humanist Category. *Critical Inquiry*, 46(1), 1–31.

Charise, Andrea. (2020). *The Aesthetics of Senescence: Aging, Population, and the Nineteenth-Century British Novel*, Albany, NY: SUNY University Press.

Charise, Andrea. (2012). "Let the Reader Think of the Burden": Old Age and the Crisis of Capacity. *Occasion: Interdisciplinary Studies in the Humanities*, 4, 1–16. http://occasion.stanford.edu/node/96.

Chase, Karen. (2009). *The Victorians and Old Age*, Oxford: Oxford University Press.

Clark, Timothy. (2016). "But the Real Problem Is... .": The Chameleonic Insidiousness of "Overpopulation" in the Environmental Humanities. *The Oxford Literary Review*, 38(1), 7–26.

Clark, Timothy. (2019). *The Value of Ecocriticism*, Cambridge: Cambridge University Press.

Coole, Diana. (2012). Reconstructing the Elderly: A Critical Analysis of Pensions and Population Policies in an Era of Demographic Ageing. *Contemporary Political Theory*, 11(1), 41–67.

Cruikshank, Margaret. (2009). *Learning To Be Old: Gender, Culture, and Aging*, Lanham, MD: Rowan and Littlefield.

Crutzen, Paul and Eugene Stoermer. (2000). The Anthropocene. *The Global Change Newsletter*, 41, 17–8.

Crutzen, Paul, Will Steffen, Jacques Grinevald, and John McNeill. (2011). The Anthropocene: Conceptual and Historical Perspectives. *Philosophical Transactions of the Royal Society*, 369, 842–67.

Csiscery-Ronay, Istvan. (2008). *The Seven Beauties of Science Fiction*, Middletown, CT: Wesleyan University Press.

Daly, Nicholas. (2015). *The Demographic Imagination and the Nineteenth-Century City: Paris, London, New York*, Cambridge: Cambridge University Press.

Davies, Jeremy. (2016). *The Birth of the Anthropocene*, Oakland, CA: University of California Press.

Davis, Janae, Alex Moulton, Levi Van Sant, and Brian Williams. (2019). Anthropocene, Capitalocene, ... Plantationocene? A Manifesto for Ecological Justice in an Age of Global Crises. *Geography Compass*, 13, 1–15.

Derrida, Jacques. (1981). *Dissemination*, translated by Barbara Johnson, Chicago, IL: University of Chicago Press.

Domingo, Andreu. (2008). "Demodystopias": Prospects of Demographic Hell. *Population and Development Review*, 34(4), 725–45.

Edelman, Lee. (2004). *No Future: Queer Theory and the Death Drive*, Durham, NC: Duke University Press.

Erdrich, Louise. (2017). *Future Home of the Living God*, London: Corsair.

Erickson, Bruce. (2010). "Fucking Close to Water": Queering the Production of the Nation. In C. Mortimer-Sandilands and B. Erickson, eds., *Queer Ecologies: Sex, Nature, Politics, Desire*, Bloomington, IN: Indiana University Press, pp. 309–30.

Falcus, Sarah. (2020). Age and Anachronism in Contemporary Dystopian Fiction. In E. Barry and M. Vide Skagen, eds., *Literature and Ageing*, Suffolk: Boydell and Brewer, pp. 65–86.

Ferris, Ina. (2002). *The Romantic National Tale and the Question of Ireland*, Cambridge: Cambridge University Press.

Freedman, Carl. (2000). *Critical Theory and Science Fiction*, Middletown, CT: Wesleyan University Press.

Furedi, Frank. (2002). Foreword. In P. Mullan, ed., *The Imaginary Time Bomb: Why an Ageing Population is Not a Social Problem*, London: Tauris, pp. xi–xvi.

Garrard, Greg. (2023). *Ecocriticism*, London: Routledge.

Garrard, Greg. (2012). Worlds without Us: Some Types of Disanthropy. *SubStance*, 127(41), 40–60.

Ghosh, Amitav. (2016). *The Great Derangement: Climate Change and the Unthinkable*, Chicago, IL: University of Chicago Press.

Gosine, Andil. (2010). Non-white Reproduction and Same-Sex Eroticism: Queer Acts against Nature. In C. Mortimer-Sandilands and B. Erickson, eds., *Queer Ecologies: Sex, Nature, Politics, Desire*, Bloomington, IN: Indiana University Press, pp. 149–72.

Grandbois, Donna. M., and Gregory. F. Sanders. (2009). The Resilience of Native American Elders. *Issues in Mental Health Nursing*, 30(9), 569–80.

Grande, Sally. (2018). Aging, Precarity, and the Struggle for Indigenous Elsewheres. *International Journal of Qualitative Studies in Education*, 31 (3), 168–76.

Grainville, Jean-Baptiste Francois Xavier Cousin de. (2002). *The Last Man*, translated by I. F. Clarke and M. Clarke, Middletown, CT: Wesleyan University Press.

Gullette, Margaret. (2004). *Aged by Culture*, Chicago, IL: University of Chicago Press.

Gullette, Margaret. (2017). *Ending Ageism, Or How Not to Shoot Old People*, Newark, NJ: Rutgers University Press.

Guterres António. (2019). Remarks to Youth Climate Summit, *United Nations*, September 21. www.un.org/sg/en/content/sg/speeches/2019-09-21/remarks-youth-climate-summit.

Halberstam, Judith. (2005). *In a Queer Time and Place: Transgender Bodies, Subcultural Lives*, New York: New York University Press.

Haq, Gary, Dave Brown, and Sarah Hards. (2010). *Older People and Climate Change: The Case for Better Engagement*, Stockholm: Stockholm Environment Institute.

Harraway, Donna. (2016a). *Staying with the Trouble: Making Kin in the Cthulucene*. Durham, NC: Duke University Press.

Harraway, Donna, Noboru Ishikawa, Scott F. Gilbert et al. (2016b). Anthropologists are Talking – about the Anthropocene. *Ethnos*, 81(3), 535–64.

Heise, Ursula. (2018). Climate Stories: Review of Amitav Ghosh's "The Great Derangement." Review of *The Great Derangement: Climate Change and the*

Unthinkable, by Amitav Ghosh, *boundary 2*, February 19. www.boundary2
.org/2018/02/ursula-k-heise-climate-stories-review-of-amitav-ghoshs-the-great-derangement/.

Heise, Ursula. (2016). *Imagining Extinction: The Cultural Meaning of Endangered Species*, Chicago, IL: University of Chicago Press.

Hejnol, Andreas. (2017). Ladders, Trees, Complexity, and Other Metaphors in Evolutionary Thinking. In N. Bubandt, E. Gan, H. Swanson, and A. Tsing, eds., *Arts of Living on a Damaged Planet*, Minneapolis, MN: University of Minnesota Press, pp. G87–G102.

Hensley, Nathan, and Philip Steer. (2019). Introduction: Ecological Formalism; or, Love among the Ruins. In N. Hensley and P. Steer, eds., *Ecological Form: System and Aesthetics in the Age of Empire*, New York: Fordham University Press, pp. 1–20.

Hulko, Wendy, Evelyn Camille, Elisabeth Antifeau et al.(2010). Views of First Nation Elders on Memory Loss and Memory Care in Later Life. *Journal of Cross-Cultural Gerontology*, 25(4), 317–42.

Ibrahim, Habiba. (2021). *Black Age: Oceanic Lifespans and the Time of Black Life*. New York: New York University Press.

James, Phyllis. D. (2018). *The Children of Men*, Croydon: Faber and Faber.

Jameson, Frederic. (2007). *Archaeologies of the Future: The Desire Called Utopia and Other Science Fictions*, New York: Verso.

Jewusiak, Jacob. (2020). *Aging, Duration, and the English Novel: Growing Old from Dickens to Woolf*, Cambridge: Cambridge University Press.

Johnson, Barbara. (1993). The Last Man. In A. Fisch, A. Mellor, and E. Schor, eds., *The Other Mary Shelley: Beyond Frankenstein*, Oxford: Oxford University Press, pp. 258–66.

Joselow, Maxine. (2023). Why Seniors are Blocking Entrances to the Four Largest U.S. Banks. *The Washington Post*, March 21. www.washington post.com/politics/2023/03/21/why-seniors-are-blocking-entrances-four-lar gest-us-banks/.

Kafer, Alison. (2013). *Feminist, Queer, Crip*, Bloomington, IN: Indiana University Press.

Katz, Stephen. (1996). *Disciplining Old Age: The Formation of Gerontological Knowledge*, Charlottesville, VA: University Press of Virginia.

King, Thomas. (1990). *All My Relations: An Anthology of Contemporary Canadian Native Fiction*, Norman, OK: University of Oklahoma Press.

LeMenager, Stephanie. (2017). Climate Change and the Struggle for Genre. In T. Menely and J. Oak Taylor, eds., *Anthropocene Reading: Literary History in Geologic Times*, Philadelphia, PA: Penn State University Press, pp. 220–38.

Lothian, Alexis. (2018). *Old Futures: Speculative Fiction and Queer Possibility*, New York: New York University Press.

Majewski, Henry. (1963). Grainville's *Le Dernier Homme*. *Symposium*, 17(2), 114–22.

Malthus, Thomas. (2015). *An Essay on the Principle of Population and Other Writings*, London: Penguin.

McGurl, Mark. (2012). The Posthuman Comedy. *Critical Inquiry*, 38(1), 533–53.

McKim, Kristi. (2022). "Always the Same and Ever New": Clouds, Aging, and Climatology. *Clouds of Sils Maria*. *ISLE: Interdisciplinary Studies in Literature and Environment*, 29(4), 1167–89.

McKusick, James. (2010). *Green Writing: Romanticism and Ecology*, London: Palgrave.

McWhir, Anne. (2002). Mary Shelley's Anti-Contagionism: The Last Man as "Fatal Narrative." *Mosaic*, 35(2), 22–38.

Mitman, Gregg, Donna Haraway, and Anna Tsing. (2019). Reflections on the Plantationocene: A conversation with Donna Haraway and Anna Tsing. *Edge Effects*, October 12, https://edgeeffects.net/haraway-tsing-plantationocene/.

Moore, Jason. (2015). *Capitalism in the Web of Life: Ecology and the Accumulation of Capital*, New York: Verso.

Morton, Timothy. (2013). *Hyperobjects: Philosophy and Ecology after the End of the World*, Minneapolis, MN: University of Minnesota Press.

Nixon, Rob. (2011). *Slow Violence and the Environmentalism of the Poor*, Cambridge, MA: Harvard University Press.

Nussbaum, Martha and Saul Levmore. (2017). *Aging Thoughtfully: Conversations about Retirement, Romance, Wrinkles, and Regret*, Oxford: Oxford University Press.

Paley, Morton. (1993). The Last Man: Apocalypse without Millennium. In A. Fisch, A. Mellor, and E. Schor, eds., *The Other Mary Shelley: Beyond Frankenstein*, Oxford: Oxford University Press, pp. 107–23.

Port, Cynthia. (2012). No Future? Aging, Temporality, History, and Reverse Chronologies. *Occasion: Interdisciplinary Studies in the Humanities*, 4, 1–19.

Psalm 90. *The Book of Common Prayer*, www.churchofengland.org/prayer-and-worship/worship-texts-and-resources/book-common-prayer/psalter/psalms-90-92.

Puar, Jasbir. (2017). *Terrorist Assemblages: Homonationalism in Queer Times*, Durham, NC: Duke University Press.

Pulido, Lauren. (2018). Racism and the Anthropocene. In G. Mitman et al., eds., *Future Remains: A Cabinet of Curiosities for the Anthropocene*, Chicago, IL: University of Chicago Press, pp. 116–28.

Said, Edward. (1983). *The World, the Text, and the Critic*, Cambridge, MA: Harvard University Press.

Sandilands, Catriona. (2004). Eco Homo: Queering the Ecological Body. *Social Philosophy Today*, 19, 17–39.

Sandilands, Catriona. (2014). Queer Life? Ecocriticism after the Fire. In G. Garrard, ed., *The Oxford Handbook of Ecocriticism*, Oxford: Oxford University Press, pp. 305–19.

Scheffler, Samuel. (2018). *Why Worry about Future Generations?* Oxford: Oxford University Press.

Sedgwick, Eve. (2003). *Touching Feeling: Affect, Pedagogy, Performativity*, Durham, NC: Duke University Press.

Seymour, Nicole. (2013). *Strange Natures: Futurity, Empathy, and the Queer Ecological Imagination*, Urbana, IL: University of Illinois Press.

Shakespeare, William. (2008). *As You Like It*, Oxford: Oxford University Press.

Sheldon, Rebekah. (2016). *The Child to Come: Life after Human Catastrophe*, Minneapolis, MN: University of Minnesota Press.

Shelley, Mary. (2008). *The Last Man*, Oxford: Oxford University Press.

Shelley, Mary. (1889). July 1823-December 1824. In J. Marshall, ed., *The Life and Letters of Mary Wollstonecraft Shelley*, Vol. II, London: Bentley.

Simpson, Leanne Betasamosake. (2021). *As We Have Always Done: Indigenous Freedom through Radical Resistance*. Minneapolis, MN: University of Minnesota Press.

Small, Helen. (2010). *The Long Life*, Oxford: Oxford University Press.

Sontag, Susan. (1972). The Double Standard of Aging. *The Saturday Review*, September 23, 29–38.

Stafford, Fiona. (1994). *The Last of the Race: The Growth of a Myth from Milton to Darwin*, Oxford: Oxford University Press.

Suvin, Darko. (1979). *Metamorphoses of Science Fiction: On the Poetics and History of a Literary Genre*, New Haven, CT: Yale University Press.

Thane, Pat. (2000). *Old Age in English History: Past Experiences, Present Issues*, Oxford: Oxford University Press.

Tsing, Anna. (2015). *The Mushroom at the End of the World: On the Possibility of Life in Capitalist Ruins*, Princeton, NJ: Princeton University Press.

Wenz, Peter and Laura Westra. (1995). Introduction. In P. Wenz and L. Westra, eds., *Faces of Environmental Racism*, New York: Rowan and Littlefield, pp. xv–xxiii.

Whyte, Kyle Powys. (2021). Time as Kinship. In J. Cohen and S. Foote, eds., *The Cambridge Companion to Environmental Humanities*, Cambridge: Cambridge University Press, pp. 39–55.

Whyte, Kyle Powys. (2020). Against Crisis Epistemology. In B. Hokowhitu, A. Moreton-Robinson, L. Tuhiwai-Smith, S. Larkin, and C. Andersen, eds., *Routledge Handbook of Critical Indigenous Studies*, New York: Routledge, pp. 52–64.

Whyte, Kyle Powys. (2017). Our Ancestors' Dystopia Now: Indigenous Conservation and the Anthropocene. In U. Heise, J. Christensen, and M. Niemann, eds., *The Routledge Companion to the Environmental Humanities*, New York: Routledge, pp. 206–15.

Willoughby, Urmi. (2021). Race, Health, and Environment. In J. Cohen and S. Foote, eds., *The Cambridge Companion to Environmental Humanities*, Cambridge: Cambridge University Press, pp. 70–85.

Wilson, Shawn. (2008). *Research is Ceremony: Indigenous Research Methods*, Halifax, CN: Fernwood.

Woods, Robert. I. (1996). The Population of Britain in the Nineteenth Century. In M. Anderson, ed., *British Population History: From the Black Death to the Present Day*, Cambridge: Cambridge University Press, pp. 281–357.

Woodward, Kathleen. (2022). "Old Trees are Our Parents": Old Growth, New Kin, Forest Time. *Age, Culture, Humanities*, 6(1), 1–29.

Woodward, Kathleen. (2020). Ageing in the Anthropocene: The View from and beyond Margaret Drabble's *The Dark Flood Rises*. In E. Barry and M. Vibe Skagen, eds., *Literature and Ageing*, Suffolk: Boydell and Brewer, pp. 37–63.

Wordsworth, William. (2002). *Selected Poetry of William Wordsworth*, New York: Modern Library.

Yusoff, Kathryn. (2018). *A Billion Black Anthropocenes or None*, Minneapolis, MN: University of Minnesota Press.

Acknowledgements

I am grateful to my colleagues at Newcastle University for their friendship and support, especially Ella Dzelzainis, Kirsten MacLeod, and Ella Mershon, who have been a constant source conviviality and stimulation. The members of the Middle Modern Writing Group at Newcastle University have listened to my weekly progress reports on the manuscript from beginning to end. My thanks to Caroline Gardner, James Harriman-Smith, and Michael Rossington for their generous comments and gentle accountability.

I greatly appreciate the feedback provided by the two anonymous reviewers of this manuscript and to Louise Westling for overseeing the project to publication. Part of the section "Queer Genre/ations" originally appeared in the journal *Poetics Today*, and I would like to thank the editors Milette Shamir and Irene Tucker for helping to refine the ideas that would eventually form the basis of this Element.

This Element is dedicated to my wife, Timea, and my daughter, Emilia. Without their constant inspiration and companionship, this Element would not exist.

Cambridge Elements ≡

Environmental Humanities

Louise Westling

University of Oregon

Louise Westling is an American scholar of literature and environmental humanities who was a founding member of the Association for the Study of Literature and Environment and its President in 1998. She has been active in the international movement for environmental cultural studies, teaching and writing on landscape imagery in literature, critical animal studies, biosemiotics, phenomenology, and deep history.

Serenella Iovino

University of North Carolina at Chapel Hill

Serenella Iovino is Professor of Italian Studies and Environmental Humanities at the University of North Carolina at Chapel Hill. She has written on a wide range of topics, including environmental ethics and ecocritical theory, bioregionalism and landscape studies, ecofeminism and posthumanism, comparative literature, eco-art, and the Anthropocene.

Timo Maran

University of Tartu

Timo Maran is an Estonian semiotician and poet. Maran is Professor of Ecosemiotics and Environmental Humanities and Head of the Department of Semiotics at the University of Tartu. His research interests are semiotic relations of nature and culture, Estonian nature writing, zoosemiotics and species conservation, and semiotics of biological mimicry.

About the Series

The environmental humanities is a new transdisciplinary complex of approaches to the embeddedness of human life and culture in all the dynamics that characterize the life of the planet. These approaches reexamine our species' history in light of the intensifying awareness of drastic climate change and ongoing mass extinction. To engage this reality, Cambridge Elements in Environmental Humanities builds on the idea of a more hybrid and participatory mode of research and debate, connecting critical and creative fields.

Cambridge Elements ≡

Environmental Humanities

Elements in the Series

A full series listing is available at: www.cambridge.org/EIEH

Printed in the United States
by Baker & Taylor Publisher Services